Contents

How to use this book

Each page has a title telling you what it is about.

Instructions look like this. Always read these carefully before starting.

This is Owl. Ask your teacher if you need to do his questions.

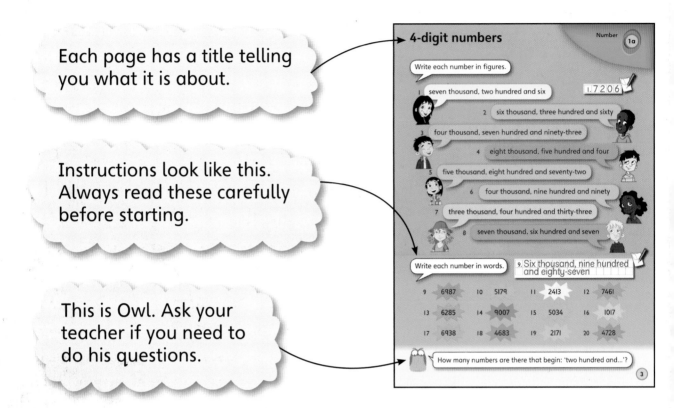

This shows you how to set out your work. The first question is done for you.

Read these word problems very carefully. Decide how you will work out the answers.

These are exploratory activities. You may like to do them with a partner.

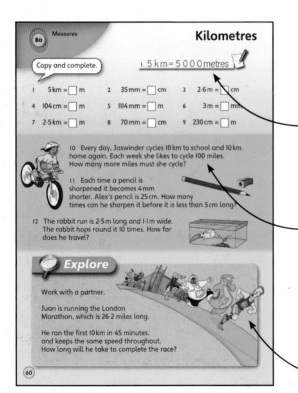

4-digit numbers

Write each number in figures.

1 seven thousand, two hundred and six

1. 7206

2 six thousand, three hundred and sixty

3 four thousand, seven hundred and ninety-three

4 eight thousand, five hundred and four

5 five thousand, eight hundred and seventy-two

6 four thousand, nine hundred and ninety

7 three thousand, four hundred and thirty-three

8 seven thousand, six hundred and seven

Write each number in words.

9. Six thousand, nine hundred and eighty-seven

9	6987	10	5179	11	2413	12	7461
13	6285	14	9007	15	5034	16	1017
17	6938	18	4683	19	2171	20	4728

How many numbers are there that begin: 'two hundred and...'?

Add the cards. Write the numbers in figures and words.

1. 8 7, 0 6 4
Eighty-seven thousand and sixty-four

1 60 7000
80 000 4

2 700 2
60 000 40
8000

3 10 000 3
3000
500 50

4 20 000 20
5000 300

5 3 100 70
40 000

6 8000 300 6
20 90 000

7 80 4000
2 70 000

8 1000 800 6
30 000

9 50 000 2 10
600 7000

Add 100 000 to each number.
Write both numbers in figures.

10. 3 6 1, 4 2 0
4 6 1, 4 2 0

10 Three hundred and sixty-one thousand, four hundred and twenty

11 Five hundred and nine thousand, six hundred and fifty-one

12 Six hundred and forty-four thousand, two hundred and thirty

13 Seven hundred and eight thousand, five hundred and forty-two

Use four 4s and up to two 0s to make
as many different numbers as possible.

5- and 6-digit numbers

> Reverse the digits each time. Write the answer in figures and words.

1   142 638   2   4244   3   620 302

4   14 104   5   5837   6   12 769

7   168 205   8   22 508   9   750 168

10 78 690   11 6032   12 874 210

1. 836,241
Eight hundred and thirty-six thousand, two hundred and forty-one

13 A factory ordered six boxes, each containing ten thousand pins, and two boxes containing one thousand pins. How many pins is this?

14 A large house costs one hundred pounds less than five hundred thousand pounds. Write the price in figures.

15 An aeroplane flies twelve thousand, six hundred and forty-two miles to Australia. It flies another thousand miles to New Zealand. How many miles has it flown in total?

16 A car had travelled ninety-nine thousand, nine hundred and ninety-nine miles. Ian drove it 10 miles to Exeter. What did the mileometer show when he arrived?

Explore

Write six different numbers between 54 999 and 60 000.
No number can use the same digit more than once!

5- and 6-digit numbers

1   Make ten different numbers larger than 10 000 using the cards below. Write each number in words and figures.

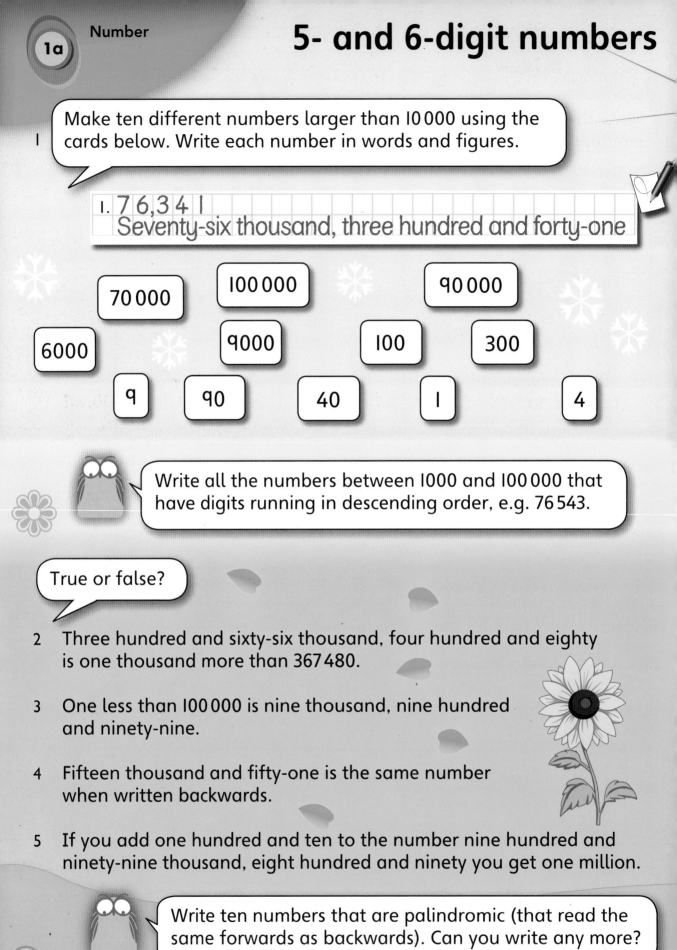

I. 7 6,3 4 I
Seventy-six thousand, three hundred and forty-one

70 000   100 000   90 000

6000   9000   100   300

9   90   40   I   4

Write all the numbers between 1000 and 100 000 that have digits running in descending order, e.g. 76 543.

True or false?

2   Three hundred and sixty-six thousand, four hundred and eighty is one thousand more than 367 480.

3   One less than 100 000 is nine thousand, nine hundred and ninety-nine.

4   Fifteen thousand and fifty-one is the same number when written backwards.

5   If you add one hundred and ten to the number nine hundred and ninety-nine thousand, eight hundred and ninety you get one million.

Write ten numbers that are palindromic (that read the same forwards as backwards). Can you write any more?

Place value

Write the value of the '3' digit in each number.

1. three hundreds
   300

1	4375	2	3758	3	4993	4	6380

5	3004	6	7030	7	5631	8	8583

9	2305	10	7430	11	3506	12	6321

Can you find ten different numbers greater than 1000, with three '5' digits in them? Can you find any more?

Write the larger of each pair of numbers in words.

13. Six thousand, four hundred and thirteen

13	4631 and 6413	14	2486 and 2475
15	3671 and 3761	16	1042 and 1102
17	5735 and 5373	18	3181 and 8131
19	8679 and 8779	20	5430 and 5340

True or false?

21 The number one larger than nine hundred and ninety-nine is ten thousand.

22 If you add 10 to one thousand and one, you get one thousand and twenty.

23 Eight thousand, nine hundred and eighty-one is nineteen less than nine thousand.

Place value

Write the value of the '7' digit in each number.

1. seventy thousand
   70,000

1	273 406	2	41 792	3	761 034
4	107 449	5	74 100	6	907 909
7	874 640	8	56 704	9	47 692
10	320 178	11	782 306	12	624 837

Write each pair of numbers in order using >.
Write the larger number in words.

13. 76,424 > 74,642
    Seventy-six thousand,
    four hundred and twenty-four

13 74 642 and 76 424   14 216 005 and 216 108

15 346 374 and 364 374   16 12 782 and 12 827

17 412 345 and 434 512   18 36 204 and 36 242

19 812 506 and 812 408   20 64 235 and 65 253

Work with a partner. You write a number. They write
a larger number, using the same digits in a different
order. Swap roles and repeat.

Place value

1 Write the number that matches each letter on the line.

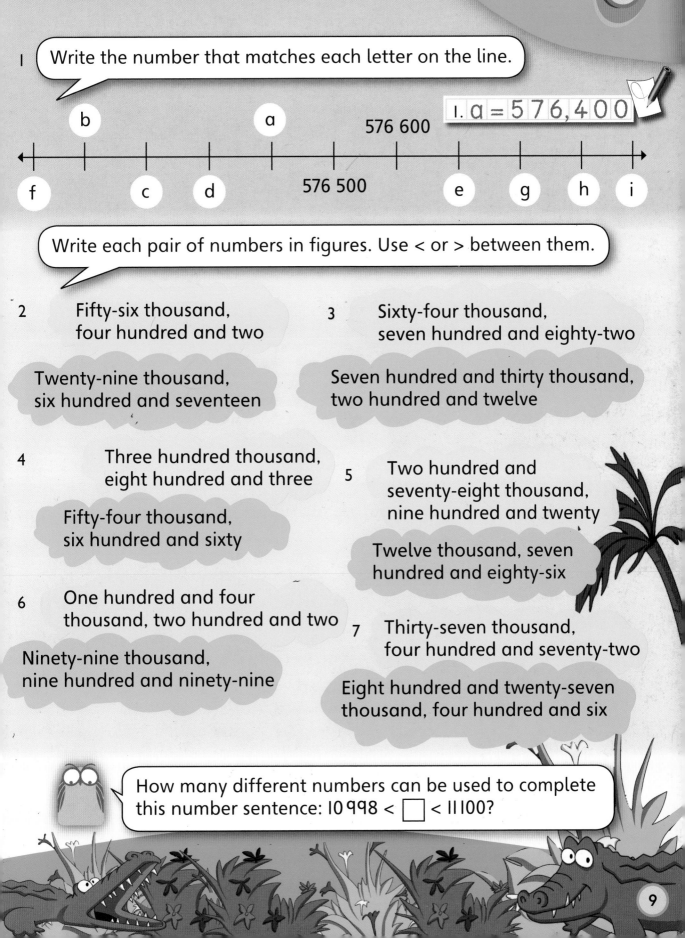

1. a = 576,400

576 600

576 500

b   a   f   c   d   e   g   h   i

Write each pair of numbers in figures. Use < or > between them.

2 Fifty-six thousand, four hundred and two

   Twenty-nine thousand, six hundred and seventeen

3 Sixty-four thousand, seven hundred and eighty-two

   Seven hundred and thirty thousand, two hundred and twelve

4 Three hundred thousand, eight hundred and three

   Fifty-four thousand, six hundred and sixty

5 Two hundred and seventy-eight thousand, nine hundred and twenty

   Twelve thousand, seven hundred and eighty-six

6 One hundred and four thousand, two hundred and two

   Ninety-nine thousand, nine hundred and ninety-nine

7 Thirty-seven thousand, four hundred and seventy-two

   Eight hundred and twenty-seven thousand, four hundred and six

How many different numbers can be used to complete this number sentence: 10 998 < ☐ < 11 100?

Place value

Write the next four numbers in each sequence.

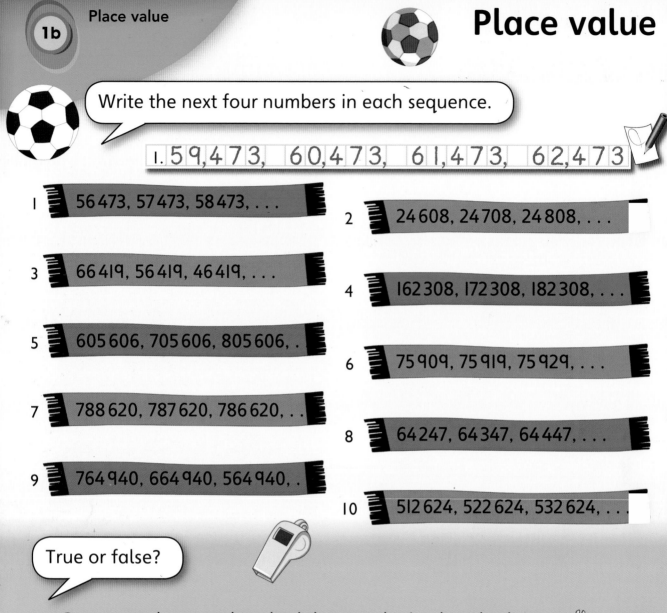

1. $\boxed{5\,9,4\,7\,3}$ $\boxed{6\,0,4\,7\,3}$ $\boxed{6\,1,4\,7\,3}$ $\boxed{6\,2,4\,7\,3}$

1   56 473, 57 473, 58 473, . . .

2   24 608, 24 708, 24 808, . . .

3   66 419, 56 419, 46 419, . . .

4   162 308, 172 308, 182 308, . . .

5   605 606, 705 606, 805 606, .

6   75 909, 75 919, 75 929, . . .

7   788 620, 787 620, 786 620, . .

8   64 247, 64 347, 64 447, . . .

9   764 940, 664 940, 564 940, .

10   512 624, 522 624, 532 624, . . .

True or false?

11   One more than one hundred thousand, nine hundred and ninety-nine is two hundred thousand.

12   Sixty thousand is halfway between sixty-one thousand, four hundred and ninety-nine, and fifty-nine thousand, five hundred.

13   919 191   <   919 199

14   One million is one more than nine hundred and ninety-nine thousand, nine hundred and ninety-nine.

How many whole numbers are there between 1 million and 2 million?

Multiplying and dividing

Complete these multiplications. Use the multiplication square to help you.

1. $4 \times 7 = 28$

1 $4 \times 7 = \square$ 2 $3 \times 9 = \square$

3 $5 \times 6 = \square$ 4 $7 \times 8 = \square$

5 $7 \times 3 = \square$ 6 $9 \times 4 = \square$

7 $6 \times 6 = \square$ 8 $2 \times 9 = \square$

9 $6 \times 8 = \square$ 10 $5 \times 7 = \square$

11 $7 \times 9 = \square$ 12 $8 \times 8 = \square$

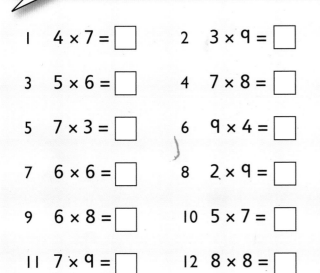

1	2	3	4	5	6	7	8	9	10
2	4	6	8	10	12	14	16	18	20
3	6	9	12	15	18	21	24	27	30
4	8	12	16	20	24	28	32	36	40
5	10	15	20	25	30	35	40	45	50
6	12	18	24	30	36	42	48	54	60
7	14	21	28	35	42	49	56	63	70
8	16	24	32	40	48	56	64	72	80
9	18	27	36	45	54	63	72	81	90
10	20	30	40	50	60	70	80	90	100

Investigate which numbers appear most often in the multiplication square.

For each machine, copy and complete the table.

13. **× 6 machine**

In	5	3	8	...
Out	30	18	...	...

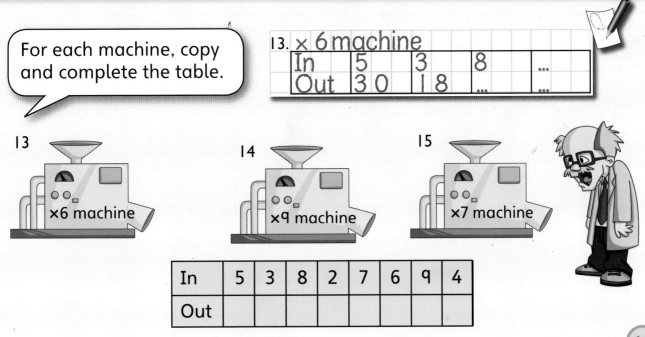

13 ×6 machine

14 ×9 machine

15 ×7 machine

In	5	3	8	2	7	6	9	4
Out								

Multiplying and dividing

Write the missing numbers.

1. 4 × 6 = 2 4

1   4 ×  = 24

2   8 × = 40

3   7 × = 28

4   6 × = 42

5   × 8 = 32

6   9 × = 36

7   6 × = 36

8   8 × = 24

9   × 5 = 45

10   × 9 = 63

Invent a missing number multiplication, whose missing number is 5. Repeat for missing numbers of 6, 7, 8 and 9.

11   Write the position of each pointer.

11. a : 21

a   b   c

0   70

d   e   f   g

0   90

h   i   j   k   l

0   60

m   n   o   p   q

0   80

Multiplying and dividing

Work out the answers to each multiplication and write the difference between the answers.

1. $5 \times 8 = 40$
   $7 \times 6 = 42$
   Difference $= 2$

1 5×8 and 7×6

2 $28 \div 4$ and $36 \div 9$

3 7×5 and 5×6

4 $56 \div 8$ and $56 \div 7$

5 8×8 and 9×9

6 3×9 and $9 \div 3$

7 $35 \div 5$ and $48 \div 6$

8 7×4 and 6×8

9 8×9 and 7×6

10 $\frac{1}{5}$ of 45 and $35 \div 7$

Invent a pair like these that has a difference of 1, of 2, ..., of 10.

Explore

Use number cards 0–9 and =, × and ×, to create matching multiplications:

$4 \times 6 = 8 \times 3$ $4 \times 5 = 2 \times 10$

How many can you find?

Write two division facts to match each multiplication.

11. $18 \div 6 = 3$
    $18 \div 3 = 6$

11 $3 \times 6 = 18$

12 $7 \times 9 = 63$

13 $8 \times 7 = 56$

14 $5 \times 9 =$

15 $4 \times 8 =$

16 $5 \times 4 =$

17 $9 \times 7 =$

18 $8 \times 6 =$

19 $5 \times 8 =$

Multiplying and dividing

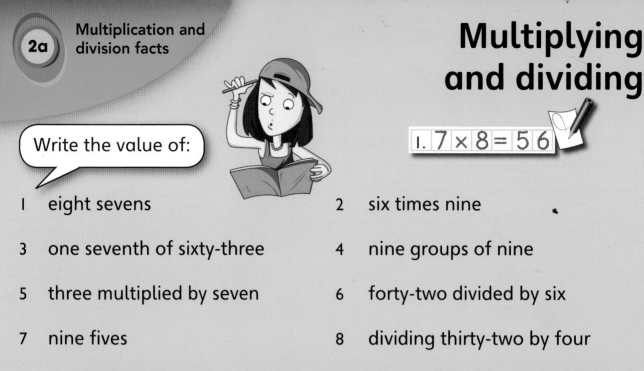

Write the value of:

1. $7 \times 8 = 56$

1	eight sevens	2	six times nine
3	one seventh of sixty-three	4	nine groups of nine
5	three multiplied by seven	6	forty-two divided by six
7	nine fives	8	dividing thirty-two by four
9	six lots of eight	10	the number of sixes in fifty-four
11	eight multiplied by itself	12	one-fifth of thirty-five

Write the missing numbers.

13. $28 \div 4 = 7$

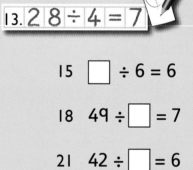

13 $28 \div \square = 7$

14 $27 \div \square = 9$

15 $\square \div 6 = 6$

16 $\square \div 7 = 5$

17 $\square \div 6 = 8$

18 $49 \div \square = 7$

19 $63 \div 9 = \square$

20 $\square \div 8 = 7$

21 $42 \div \square = 6$

Explore

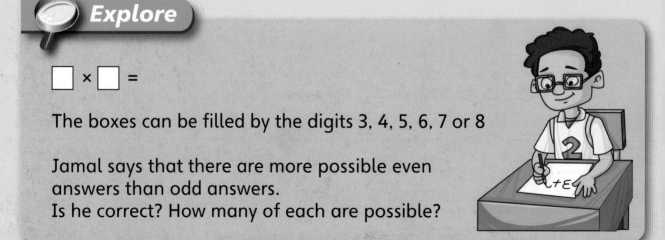

$\square \times \square =$

The boxes can be filled by the digits 3, 4, 5, 6, 7 or 8

Jamal says that there are more possible even answers than odd answers.
Is he correct? How many of each are possible?

Remainders as whole numbers

Complete the divisions, showing the remainders. Use the square to help you.

1. 7 r 3

1	2	3	4	5	6	7	8	9	10
2	4	6	8	10	12	14	16	18	20
3	6	9	12	15	18	21	24	27	30
4	8	12	16	20	24	28	32	36	40
5	10	15	20	25	30	35	40	45	50
6	12	18	24	30	36	42	48	54	60
7	14	21	28	35	42	49	56	63	70
8	16	24	32	40	48	56	64	72	80
9	18	27	36	45	54	63	72	81	90
10	20	30	40	50	60	70	80	90	100

1   31 ÷ 4

2   17 ÷ 2

3   31 ÷ 9

4   46 ÷ 10

5   37 ÷ 6

6   26 ÷ 3

7   43 ÷ 8

8   18 ÷ 4

9   27 ÷ 7

10   42 ÷ 5

11   34 ÷ 5

12   27 ÷ 4

Use the square to help you write some divisions that have a remainder of 4.

The sports shop is having a stock take. How many boxes of each are there, and how many left over?

13. 53 ÷ 6 = 8 boxes   r 5

13   53 golf balls

boxes of 6

14   47 tennis balls

boxes of 5

15   89 ping pong balls

boxes of 10

16   26 cricket balls

boxes of 3

17   31 squash balls

boxes of 7

18   53 shuttlecocks

boxes of 8

If the shop has 100 of each type of ball, which will fill the boxes exactly, with no remainder?

Remainders as fractions and decimals

Each envelope needs a stamp. Write how many books of 10 stamps are needed. Write the remainders as (a) a fraction and (b) a decimal.

1. 3 books
(a) $2\frac{3}{10}$ (b) 2.3

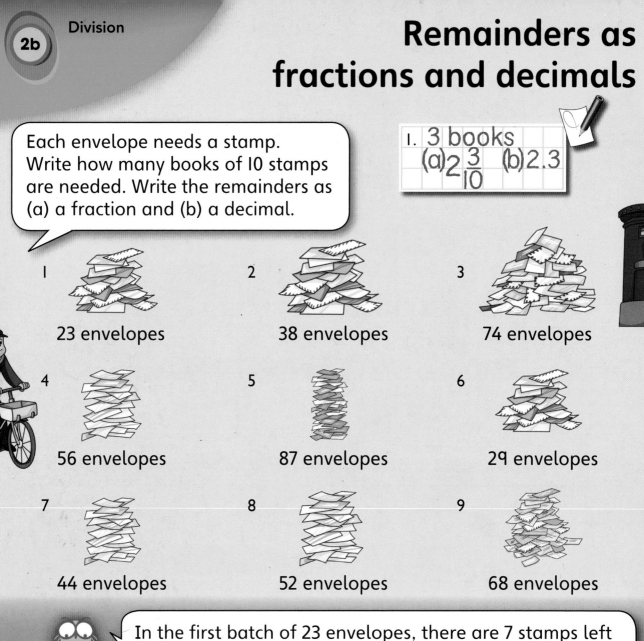

1 23 envelopes

2 38 envelopes

3 74 envelopes

4 56 envelopes

5 87 envelopes

6 29 envelopes

7 44 envelopes

8 52 envelopes

9 68 envelopes

In the first batch of 23 envelopes, there are 7 stamps left in a book. Find how many left-over stamps there are each time. Add them up. What size book would you design to package these stamps in the most efficient way?

Complete each division, writing the remainders as fractions.

10. $18 \div 5 = 3\frac{3}{5}$

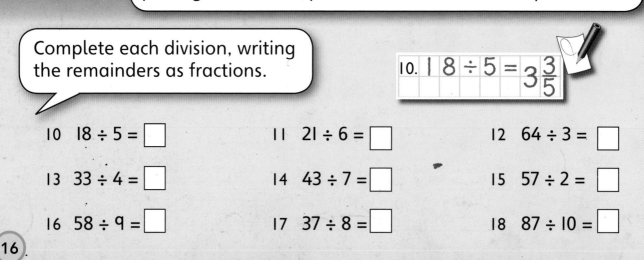

10 $18 \div 5 = \boxed{}$

11 $21 \div 6 = \boxed{}$

12 $64 \div 3 = \boxed{}$

13 $33 \div 4 = \boxed{}$

14 $43 \div 7 = \boxed{}$

15 $57 \div 2 = \boxed{}$

16 $58 \div 9 = \boxed{}$

17 $37 \div 8 = \boxed{}$

18 $87 \div 10 = \boxed{}$

Remainders

> Complete the divisions, writing each remainder as a decimal.

1. | 3 · 1 |

1. 31 ÷ 10
2. 76 ÷ 10
3. 43 ÷ 2
4. 81 ÷ 2

5. 17 ÷ 4
6. 33 ÷ 4
7. 12 ÷ 5
8. 28 ÷ 5

9. 28 ÷ 20
10. 34 ÷ 4
11. 32 ÷ 5
12. 47 ÷ 5

13. 31 children are given an apple each. How many bags of 5 apples are needed?

14. 37 racing pigeons are split into teams of 3. How many teams are there?

15. Taxis can take 4 passengers. How many taxis are needed to transport a class of 26 children and their teacher to the station?

16. Flights to Paris cost £52. How many flight tickets can be bought with £380?

17. > Copy and complete the table.

Divide by	27	33	81	55	103
10	2·7				
2	13·5				
4					
5					

Write the cost of one of each raffle ticket.

1. £4·50 ÷ 10 = £0·45

1. Win a teddy!

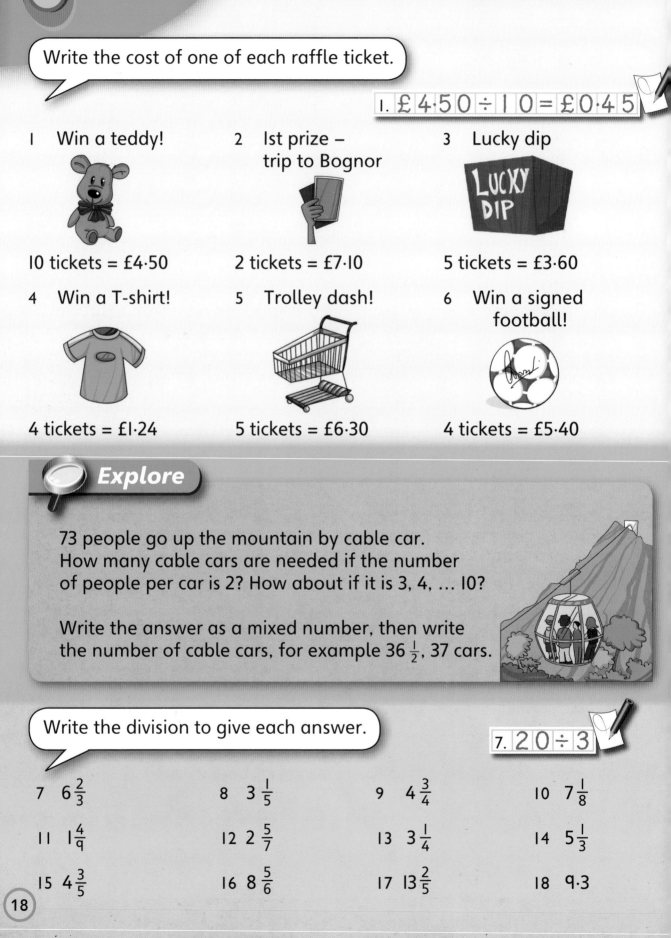

10 tickets = £4·50

2. 1st prize – trip to Bognor

2 tickets = £7·10

3. Lucky dip

LUCKY DIP

5 tickets = £3·60

4. Win a T-shirt!

4 tickets = £1·24

5. Trolley dash!

5 tickets = £6·30

6. Win a signed football!

4 tickets = £5·40

🔍 Explore

73 people go up the mountain by cable car.
How many cable cars are needed if the number
of people per car is 2? How about if it is 3, 4, … 10?

Write the answer as a mixed number, then write
the number of cable cars, for example $36\frac{1}{2}$, 37 cars.

Write the division to give each answer.

7. 20 ÷ 3

7. $6\frac{2}{3}$

8. $3\frac{1}{5}$

9. $4\frac{3}{4}$

10. $7\frac{1}{8}$

11. $1\frac{4}{9}$

12. $2\frac{5}{7}$

13. $3\frac{1}{4}$

14. $5\frac{1}{3}$

15. $4\frac{3}{5}$

16. $8\frac{5}{6}$

17. $13\frac{2}{5}$

18. 9·3

Doubling

Double each part and write a double for the total.

1. Double 3 7 = 6 0 + 1 4 = 7 4

1   3 0
        7

2   2
      4 0

3   3
      7 0

4   2 0
    8

5   4
      8 0

6   5 0
        7

7   6 0
    q

8   6
      7 0

9   7
      q 0

10 Chang has collected 75 2p coins. How much does he have in total?

11 Leo watches 4 programmes of 45 minutes each. For how many hours and minutes does he watch TV?

Write the number of gloves in each box.

12. Double 3 4 = 6 0 + 8 = 6 8

12 34 pairs

13 42 pairs

14 53 pairs

15 62 pairs

16 76 pairs

17 88 pairs

18 47 pairs

19 39 pairs

20 97 pairs

Choose two boxes. If each glove has 4 fingers, use doubling to find the number of fingers in the boxes.

Doubling and halving

Cycle trips

Write the total distance there and back.

1. Double 7·6 = 14 + 1·2 = 15·2 km

1 To Bishop's Castle 7·6 km

2 To Canoe Lake 8·4 km

3 To Primrose Wood 6·8 km

4 To Stony Beach 5·9 km

5 To Bell Tower 7·3 km

6 To Dream River 2·8 km

7 To Craggy Rock 4·7 km

8 To Bat Cavern 3·6 km

9 To Old Chapel 7·9 km

Sita made two cycle trips over the weekend. The total distance she cycled was between 30 km and 32 km. Which of these trips could she have done?

Write the number coming out of the machine when these are put in.

10 84

11 68

12 46

13 98

14 74

15 126

16 142

17 138

18 154

19 176

20 192

21 108

Halving Machine

Doubling and halving

These are the total journeys there and back. Write how far away each place is.

1. Half of 14·2 = 7·0 + 0·1 = 7·1 km

1 14·2 km

2 12·8 km

3 16·4 km

4 18·2 km

5 10·6 km

6 11·8 km

7 17·8 km

8 15·4 km

9 13·6 km

These are ferry prices to different islands. Child tickets are half price.

Andros £36   Hydra £78   Santorini £86   Naxos £62   Paros £54   Tinos £48

Find the cost of the following tickets.

1 adult and 1 child to   10 Naxos   11 Santorini   12 Andros

2 adults and 1 child to   13 Tinos   14 Hydra   15 Paros

2 adults and 3 children to 16 Andros   17 Tinos   18 Naxos

Find which is the cheapest to Naxos: 2 adults and 3 children, 3 adults and 1 child or 1 adult and 5 children. Write a question like this for your friend to answer.

Doubling and halving

Copy and complete.

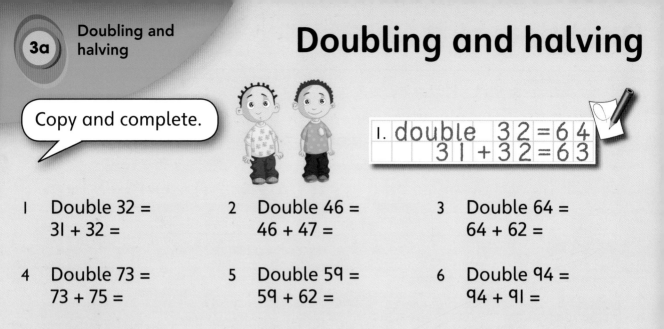

1. double $32 = 64$
   $31 + 32 = 63$

1 Double 32 =
   31 + 32 =

2 Double 46 =
   46 + 47 =

3 Double 64 =
   64 + 62 =

4 Double 73 =
   73 + 75 =

5 Double 59 =
   59 + 62 =

6 Double 94 =
   94 + 91 =

7 Double 7·3 =
   7·3 + 7·5 =

8 Double 8·6 =
   8·8 + 8·6 =

9 Double 3·2 =
   3·2 + 3·3 =

10 Double 6·2 =
    6·2 + 6·4 =

11 Double 5·5 =
    5·5 + 5·4 =

12 Double 4·3 =
    4·3 + 4·2 =

Find numbers to put in these boxes: Double ☐ is half of ☐

I am a number. Who am I?

13 Half of me is double 34.

14 Double me is half of 144.

15 I am 38 more than half of 126.

16 I am 75 less than double 64.

17 When I am doubled, then
    doubled again, the answer is 192.

18 When I am halved, then halved
    again, the answer is double 26.

19 Half of me is double 14.

20 I am 28 more than double 14.

Invent a 'Who am I?' question using doubling and halving.

Doubling

Double each part and write a double for the total.

1. Double 460 = 800 + 120 = 920

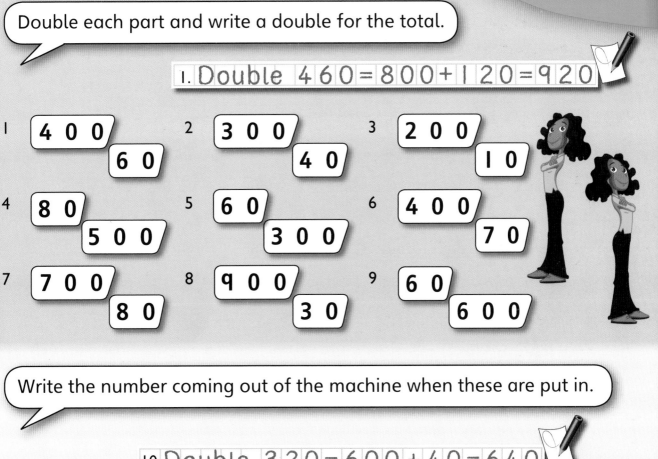

1. 400 / 60
2. 300 / 40
3. 200 / 10
4. 80 / 500
5. 60 / 300
6. 400 / 70
7. 700 / 80
8. 900 / 30
9. 60 / 600

Write the number coming out of the machine when these are put in.

10. Double 320 = 600 + 40 = 640

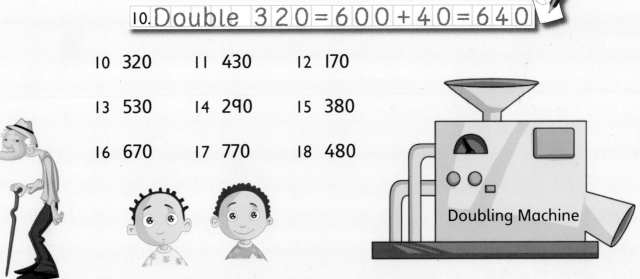

10	320	11	430	12	170
13	530	14	290	15	380
16	670	17	770	18	480

Doubling Machine

Choose a multiple of 10, e.g. 30. Put it in the machine (60). Put this back in the machine (120). Keep going – how many times can you do this?

Doubling

Football programmes cost £2 each. Write how much is collected when these programmes are sold.

1. $3700 \times £2 = £6000 + £1400$
$= £7400$

1	3700 programmes	2	4800 programmes	3	2300 programmes
4	5500 programmes	5	7400 programmes	6	6700 programmes
7	8300 programmes	8	9800 programmes	9	3900 programmes

 If the programmes cost £2·50, find a quick way of working out the new amounts collected.

Write how many £2 programmes are sold by these clubs:

10. Half of $£6800 = £3000 + £400$
$= £3400$

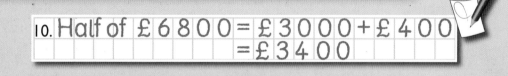

10	Rovers £6800	11	City £7500	12	Town £9400
13	Athletic £13200	14	Albion £18700	15	Rangers £17900

 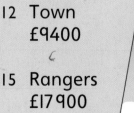 

Doubling

Write the cost of two of each T-shirt.

1. Double £6·20 = £12 + 40p
                = £12·40

1 £6·20 each

2 £7·40 each

3 £3·10 each

4 £5·30 each

5 £9·60 each

6 £4·90 each

7 £8·70 each

8 £6·80 each

9 £12·70 each

Find the cost of four of each T-shirt by doubling.

If I bought two of one type of T-shirt with a £10 note, and received one silver coin in change, what could the price of the T-shirt be?

10 Joe has 730 boxes of chocolates to sell at the market. He sold half of them for £2 a box, and the others at half price. How much money did he make?

11 Rachel has saved some money. When her aunt has doubled it, then her granny doubled this again, she has £28·40. How much did she start with?

12 Ling saved £6·40 and Mai saved £4·70. Their dad doubled their savings. How much did they have between them?

13 Afram flies 560 km to Rome and back. How far does he fly? He does this each weekend for a month. How far does he fly in total?

Halving

Write the sale price for each DVD.

1. Half of £14·60 = £7·30

DVDs half price!

1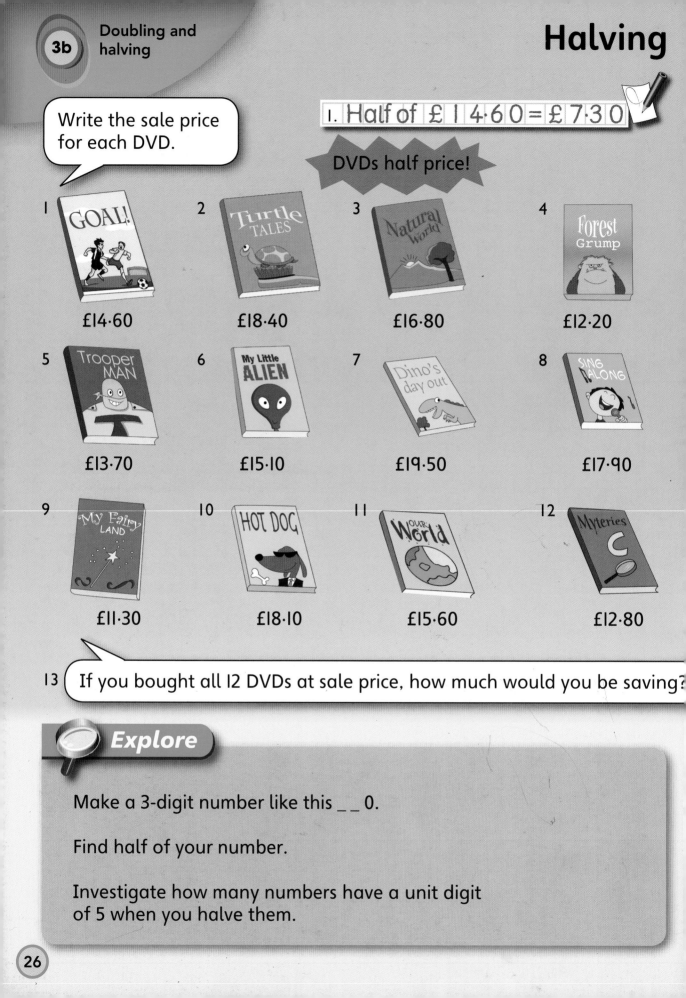
£14·60

2
£18·40

3
£16·80

4
£12·20

5
£13·70

6
£15·10

7
£19·50

8
£17·90

9
£11·30

10
£18·10

11
£15·60

12
£12·80

13 If you bought all 12 DVDs at sale price, how much would you be saving?

Explore

Make a 3-digit number like this _ _ 0.

Find half of your number.

Investigate how many numbers have a unit digit of 5 when you halve them.

Improper fractions and mixed numbers

Write the number of slices in each set.

1. $\dfrac{9}{4}$

1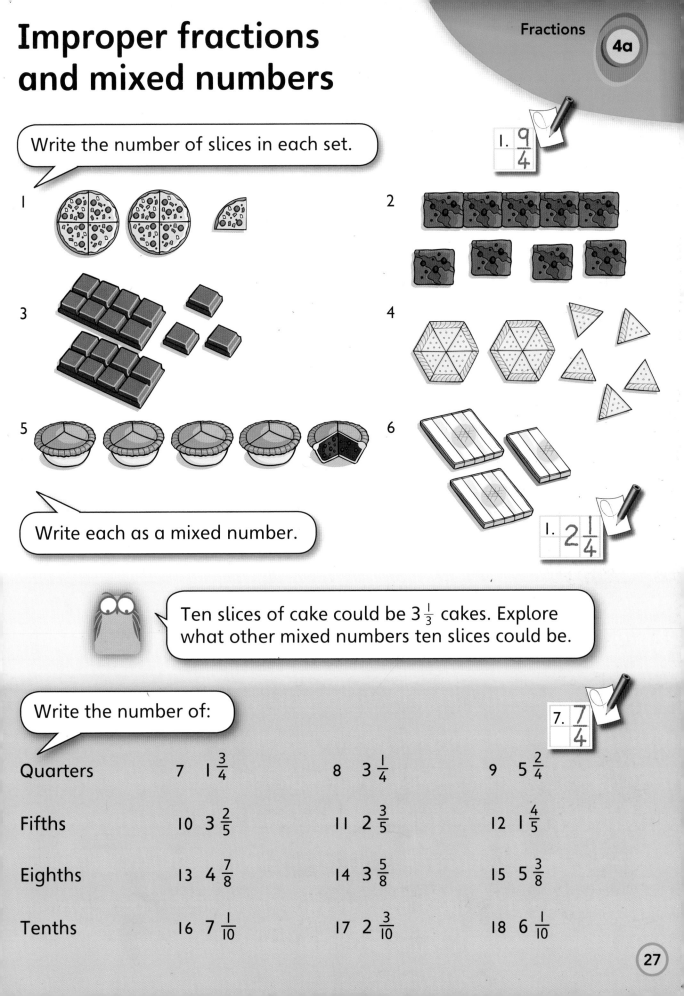

2

3

4

5

6

1. $2\dfrac{1}{4}$

Write each as a mixed number.

Ten slices of cake could be $3\dfrac{1}{3}$ cakes. Explore what other mixed numbers ten slices could be.

Write the number of:

7. $\dfrac{7}{4}$

Quarters	7 $1\dfrac{3}{4}$	8 $3\dfrac{1}{4}$	9 $5\dfrac{2}{4}$
Fifths	10 $3\dfrac{2}{5}$	11 $2\dfrac{3}{5}$	12 $1\dfrac{4}{5}$
Eighths	13 $4\dfrac{7}{8}$	14 $3\dfrac{5}{8}$	15 $5\dfrac{3}{8}$
Tenths	16 $7\dfrac{1}{10}$	17 $2\dfrac{3}{10}$	18 $6\dfrac{1}{10}$

Improper fractions and mixed numbers

Write each as a mixed number.

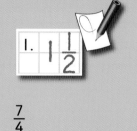

1. $1\frac{1}{2}$

1 $\dfrac{3}{2}$ 2 $\dfrac{4}{3}$ 3 $\dfrac{7}{4}$ 4 $\dfrac{13}{10}$

5 $\dfrac{13}{5}$ 6 $\dfrac{21}{8}$ 7 $\dfrac{17}{7}$ 8 $\dfrac{50}{6}$

Explore

Use number cards 2–8.

Choose two cards to make an improper fraction that can also be written as a mixed number:

$$\frac{7}{5} = 1\frac{2}{5}$$

Watch out! $\frac{6}{2}$ will not do, because it cannot make a mixed number.

How many improper fractions like this can you make?

Write the number of towers of each height.

9. $2\frac{3}{5}$

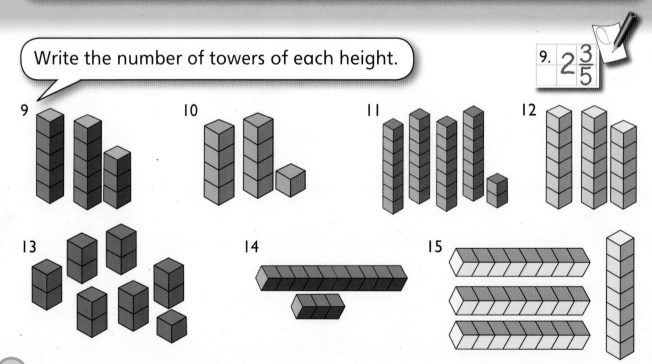

9   10   11   12

13   14   15

Improper fractions and mixed numbers

Write <, > or = between each pair.

1. $3\frac{1}{2} < \frac{9}{2}$

1 $3\frac{1}{2}$ and $\frac{9}{2}$ 2 $4\frac{2}{3}$ and $\frac{16}{3}$ 3 $\frac{27}{4}$ and $5\frac{3}{4}$

4 $\frac{21}{5}$ and $3\frac{4}{5}$ 5 $3\frac{7}{10}$ and $\frac{31}{10}$ 6 $\frac{23}{6}$ and $3\frac{5}{6}$

7 $\frac{38}{7}$ and $5\frac{2}{7}$ 8 $\frac{59}{9}$ and $6\frac{7}{9}$ 9 $4\frac{3}{8}$ and $\frac{31}{8}$ 10 $2\frac{5}{12}$ and $\frac{29}{12}$

Change each set to mixed numbers, then write them in order, smallest to largest:

11 $\frac{7}{3}$, $\frac{7}{4}$, $\frac{5}{2}$, $\frac{21}{5}$, $\frac{53}{10}$ 12 $\frac{23}{6}$, $\frac{21}{5}$, $\frac{27}{10}$, $\frac{16}{3}$, $\frac{27}{4}$

13 $\frac{8}{9}$, $\frac{10}{7}$, $\frac{14}{3}$, $\frac{29}{8}$, $\frac{14}{5}$ 14 $\frac{33}{4}$, $\frac{38}{7}$, $\frac{38}{9}$, $\frac{63}{10}$, $\frac{13}{8}$

15 $\frac{11}{4}$, $\frac{23}{3}$, $\frac{17}{5}$, $\frac{9}{2}$, $\frac{35}{6}$ 16 $\frac{24}{5}$, $\frac{18}{7}$, $\frac{17}{10}$, $\frac{29}{4}$, $\frac{26}{3}$

Write a set of improper fractions whose mixed numbers are between 5 and 10.

I am a fraction. Who am I?

17 My numerator and denominator have a total of 7. I am between $\frac{1}{2}$ and 1.

18 My denominator is double my numerator. I am a number of sixths.

19 I am between 2 and 3 and my denominator is 2.

20 My numerator and denominator have a total of 10. I am between 2 and 3.

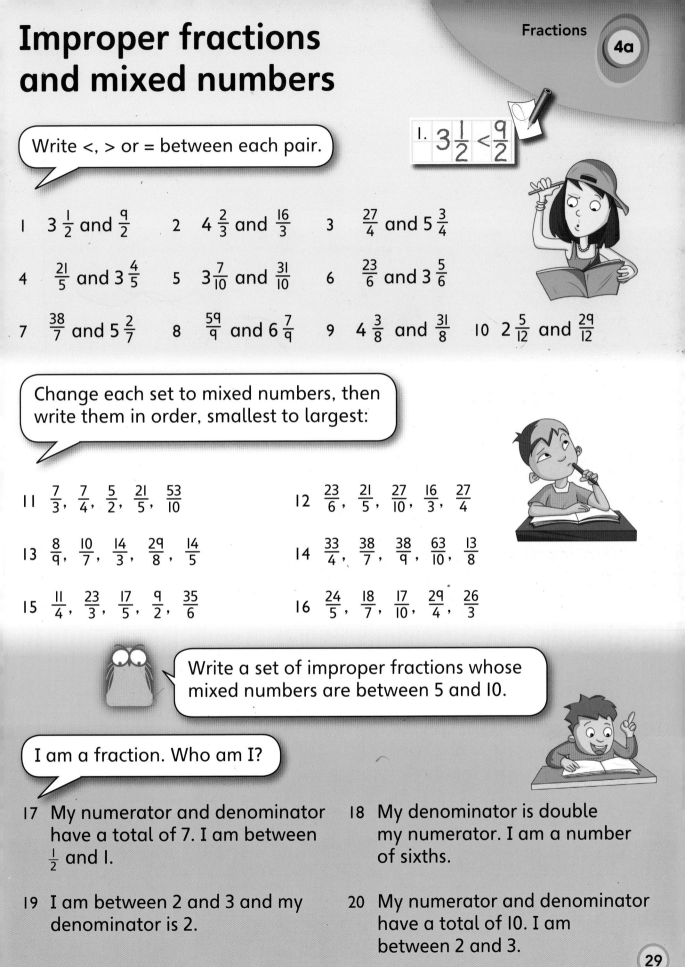

Improper fractions and mixed numbers

Write each time as a fraction of an hour.

1. $\frac{1}{3}$ hour

1

2

3

Write these times in hours.

4. $1\frac{1}{4}$ hours

4   75 minutes

5   90 minutes

6   210 minutes

7   80 minutes

8   160 minutes

9   85 minutes

10 630 minutes

11 320 minutes

12 65 minutes

Write the number of minutes in:

13. $2\frac{3}{4}$ hours

14 $3\frac{7}{12}$ hours

15 $5\frac{2}{3}$ hours

16 $4\frac{1}{12}$ hours

17 $2\frac{2}{3}$ hours

18 $7\frac{5}{6}$ hours

Explore

150 minutes $= 2\frac{1}{2}$ hours

190 minutes $= 3\frac{1}{6}$ hours

Investigate how many mixed numbers of hours you can write between 100 and 200 minutes.

Equivalent fractions

For each set of pictures, write a set of equivalent fractions.

1. $\dfrac{1}{2}, \dfrac{2}{4} \ldots$

Find the equivalent fractions. Use the 10 × 10 square to help you.

6 $\dfrac{60}{100} = \dfrac{\Box}{10}$

7 $\dfrac{1}{2} = \dfrac{\Box}{10}$

8 $\dfrac{1}{2} = \dfrac{\Box}{100}$

9 $\dfrac{10}{100} = \dfrac{\Box}{10}$

10 $\dfrac{9}{10} = \dfrac{\Box}{100}$

11 $\dfrac{1}{4} = \dfrac{\Box}{100}$

12 $\dfrac{3}{4} = \dfrac{\Box}{100}$

13 $\dfrac{4}{10} = \dfrac{\Box}{100}$

Write equivalent fractions for each of $\dfrac{1}{10}$, $\dfrac{2}{10}$, $\ldots \dfrac{2}{10}$.
Can you write some for twentieths?

Equivalent fractions

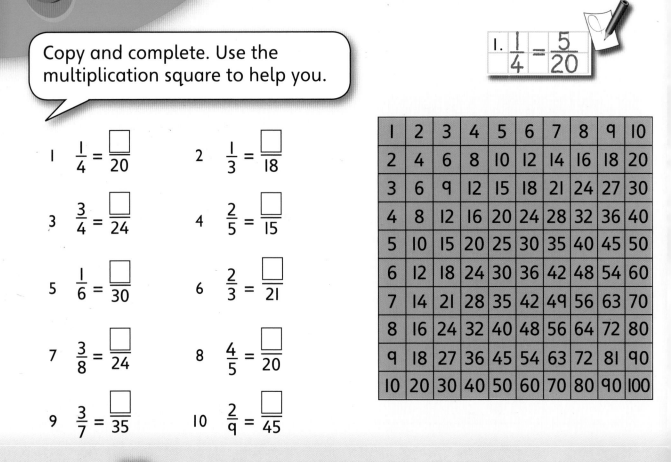

Copy and complete. Use the multiplication square to help you.

1. $\dfrac{1}{4} = \dfrac{5}{20}$

1   $\dfrac{1}{4} = \dfrac{\square}{20}$ 2 $\dfrac{1}{3} = \dfrac{\square}{18}$

3   $\dfrac{3}{4} = \dfrac{\square}{24}$ 4 $\dfrac{2}{5} = \dfrac{\square}{15}$

5   $\dfrac{1}{6} = \dfrac{\square}{30}$ 6 $\dfrac{2}{3} = \dfrac{\square}{21}$

7   $\dfrac{3}{8} = \dfrac{\square}{24}$ 8 $\dfrac{4}{5} = \dfrac{\square}{20}$

9   $\dfrac{3}{7} = \dfrac{\square}{35}$ 10 $\dfrac{2}{9} = \dfrac{\square}{45}$

1	2	3	4	5	6	7	8	9	10
2	4	6	8	10	12	14	16	18	20
3	6	9	12	15	18	21	24	27	30
4	8	12	16	20	24	28	32	36	40
5	10	15	20	25	30	35	40	45	50
6	12	18	24	30	36	42	48	54	60
7	14	21	28	35	42	49	56	63	70
8	16	24	32	40	48	56	64	72	80
9	18	27	36	45	54	63	72	81	90
10	20	30	40	50	60	70	80	90	100

Write as many pairs of equivalent fractions as you can that contain the digit 3.

Write how many:

11. $\dfrac{6}{8}$

Eighths   11 $\dfrac{3}{4}$ 12 $\dfrac{1}{2}$ 13 $\dfrac{1}{4}$

Tenths   14 $\dfrac{70}{100}$ 15 $\dfrac{3}{5}$ 16 $\dfrac{1}{2}$

Sixths   17 $\dfrac{10}{12}$ 18 $\dfrac{2}{3}$ 19 $\dfrac{50}{60}$

Hundredths   20 $\dfrac{7}{10}$ 21 $\dfrac{3}{4}$ 22 $\dfrac{3}{20}$

Equivalent fractions

Copy and complete. Use the lines to help you.

1. $\dfrac{1}{4} = \dfrac{2}{8}$

0 —— $\dfrac{1}{2}$ —— 1

0 —— $\dfrac{1}{4}$ —— $\dfrac{2}{4}$ —— $\dfrac{3}{4}$ —— 1

0 — $\dfrac{1}{8}$ — $\dfrac{2}{8}$ — $\dfrac{3}{8}$ — $\dfrac{4}{8}$ — $\dfrac{5}{8}$ — $\dfrac{6}{8}$ — $\dfrac{7}{8}$ — 1

1 $\quad \dfrac{1}{4} = \dfrac{\square}{8}$ $\qquad$ 2 $\quad \dfrac{1}{2} = \dfrac{\square}{4}$

3 $\quad \dfrac{4}{8} = \dfrac{\square}{4}$ $\qquad$ 4 $\quad \dfrac{3}{4} = \dfrac{\square}{8}$

5 $\quad \dfrac{1}{2} = \dfrac{\square}{8}$

0 —— $\dfrac{1}{3}$ —— $\dfrac{2}{3}$ —— 1

0 —— $\dfrac{1}{4}$ —— $\dfrac{2}{4}$ —— $\dfrac{3}{4}$ —— 1

0 —— $\dfrac{6}{12}$ —— 1

6 $\quad \dfrac{1}{3} = \dfrac{\square}{6}$ $\qquad$ 7 $\quad \dfrac{3}{6} = \dfrac{\square}{12}$

8 $\quad \dfrac{1}{6} = \dfrac{\square}{12}$ $\qquad$ 9 $\quad \dfrac{2}{3} = \dfrac{\square}{12}$

10 $\quad \dfrac{4}{6} = \dfrac{\square}{3}$ $\qquad$ 11 $\quad \dfrac{5}{6} = \dfrac{\square}{12}$

Use these lines to write some pairs of equivalent fractions:

0 —— $\dfrac{1}{2}$ —— 1

0 —— $\dfrac{1}{5}$ —— $\dfrac{2}{5}$ —— $\dfrac{3}{5}$ —— $\dfrac{4}{5}$ —— 1

0 —— $\dfrac{5}{10}$ —— 1

12 Write pairs of letters for the equivalent fractions.

12. A and . . .

A	B	C	D	E	F	G
$\dfrac{2}{6}$	$\dfrac{3}{5}$	$\dfrac{3}{4}$	$\dfrac{1}{2}$	$\dfrac{2}{10}$	$\dfrac{1}{4}$	$\dfrac{1}{3}$

H	I	J	K	L	M	N
$\dfrac{2}{3}$	$\dfrac{6}{8}$	$\dfrac{1}{5}$	$\dfrac{2}{4}$	$\dfrac{4}{6}$	$\dfrac{2}{8}$	$\dfrac{6}{10}$

13 Write another equivalent fraction for each pair.

Equivalent fractions

> I am a fraction. Who am I?

1 I am equivalent to two-thirds. My denominator is 12.

2 I am equivalent to three-quarters. My numerator is 6.

3 I am equivalent to one-third. My numerator and denominator have a total of 12.

4 I am equivalent to four-fifths. My denominator is 20.

> Copy and complete.

5. $0.7 = \dfrac{7}{10} = \dfrac{14}{20}$

5 $0.7 = \dfrac{\square}{10} = \dfrac{\square}{20}$

6 $0.5 = \dfrac{\square}{10} = \dfrac{\square}{100}$

7 $0.25 = \dfrac{\square}{100} = \dfrac{\square}{4}$

8 $0.08 = \dfrac{\square}{100} = \dfrac{\square}{50}$

9 $1.6 = \dfrac{\square}{10} = \dfrac{\square}{5}$

10 $0.8 = \dfrac{\square}{10} = \dfrac{\square}{5}$

11 $2.4 = \dfrac{\square}{10} = \dfrac{\square}{100}$

Explore

Use number cards 1–20.

Here is a set of three equivalent fractions: $\dfrac{1}{3}$, $\dfrac{2}{6}$, $\dfrac{4}{12}$

Investigate other sets of three equivalent fractions.

Can you find a set of four?

Can you find a set of more than four?

Equivalent fractions

Use the number lines to help you.

Write a fraction:

1 greater than $\frac{3}{4}$

2 less than $\frac{1}{3}$

3 less than $\frac{1}{5}$

4 greater than $\frac{1}{2}$

5 equivalent to $\frac{3}{5}$

6 greater than $\frac{2}{3}$

7 between $\frac{1}{2}$ and $\frac{3}{4}$

8 equivalent to $\frac{1}{2}$

9 greater than $\frac{1}{5}$

10 between $\frac{2}{12}$ and $\frac{8}{12}$

11 between $\frac{2}{5}$ and $\frac{4}{5}$

12 between $\frac{5}{12}$ and $\frac{7}{12}$

13 equivalent to $\frac{10}{12}$

14 equivalent to $\frac{2}{5}$

1. (c) $\frac{11}{12}$

How many fractions can you find that are between $\frac{1}{4}$ and $\frac{3}{4}$, where the denominator is 8 or less?

Ordering fractions

5a

Write the fraction, and an equivalent fraction for it.

1. (a) $\frac{6}{12} = \frac{1}{2}$

| h | f | b | d | | a | | e | f | c | g |

0 —— 1

Use the line to help you write < or > between each pair of fractions.

2. $\frac{1}{2} = \frac{6}{12}$
$\frac{1}{2} < \frac{7}{12}$

0 —— 1

2 $\frac{1}{2}$, $\frac{7}{12}$ 3 $\frac{5}{6}$, $\frac{2}{3}$ 4 $\frac{3}{4}$, $\frac{11}{12}$ 5 $\frac{1}{3}$, $\frac{1}{4}$

0 —— 1

6 $\frac{4}{5}$, $\frac{9}{10}$ 7 $\frac{13}{20}$, $\frac{3}{5}$ 8 $\frac{3}{4}$, $\frac{4}{5}$ 9 $\frac{1}{4}$, $\frac{9}{20}$

Write < or > between each pair of fractions.

MATHS

10 $\frac{5}{8}$, $\frac{1}{2}$ 11 $\frac{6}{15}$, $\frac{1}{3}$ 12 $\frac{4}{5}$, $\frac{18}{20}$

13 $\frac{1}{2}$, $\frac{7}{16}$ 14 $\frac{3}{8}$, $\frac{1}{4}$ 15 $\frac{7}{15}$, $\frac{13}{30}$

Draw a number line with 16 marks. Mark these fractions on it:

16 $\frac{1}{16}$ 17 $\frac{1}{2}$ 18 $\frac{3}{8}$ 19 $\frac{3}{4}$

20 $\frac{7}{8}$ 21 $\frac{15}{16}$ 22 $\frac{1}{4}$ 23 $\frac{5}{8}$

Use a line marked in 10ths and one marked in 12ths. With a partner, choose a different line each. Select a fraction on your line and compare them. Write them in order, using > or =. Repeat.

Ordering fractions

Write these in order.

1. $\frac{3}{4}$, $1\frac{3}{4}$, $2\frac{1}{4}$, $2\frac{1}{2}$

1 $2\frac{1}{2}$, $2\frac{1}{4}$, $1\frac{3}{4}$, $\frac{3}{4}$

2 $3\frac{1}{2}$, $4\frac{1}{5}$, $3\frac{7}{10}$, $4\frac{1}{2}$, $3\frac{2}{5}$

3 $1\frac{1}{8}$, $1\frac{5}{8}$, $2\frac{1}{4}$, $1\frac{1}{4}$, $2\frac{3}{8}$, $2\frac{1}{2}$

4 $1\frac{1}{6}$, $1\frac{8}{12}$, $2\frac{5}{6}$, $2\frac{1}{12}$, $\frac{5}{6}$

Find the fractions of eggs. Write the fractions in each row in order.

5. $\frac{3}{4}$ of 36 = 27 eggs

36 eggs

5 $\frac{3}{4}$ 6 $\frac{5}{6}$ 7 $\frac{4}{9}$ 8 $\frac{1}{2}$

40 eggs

9 $\frac{2}{5}$ 10 $\frac{3}{8}$ 11 $\frac{7}{10}$ 12 $\frac{3}{4}$

48 eggs

13 $\frac{5}{6}$ 14 $\frac{5}{8}$ 15 $\frac{3}{4}$ 16 $\frac{7}{12}$

I have 72 eggs. Write two fractions with different denominators that can be made from this number, e.g. $\frac{3}{4}$ and $\frac{1}{6}$. What other fractions can be made from 72 eggs?

Ordering fractions

Write < or > between each pair of fractions.

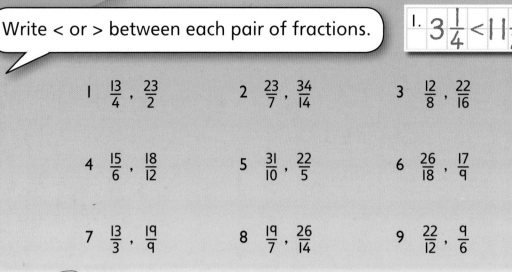

1. $3\frac{1}{4} < 11\frac{1}{2}$

1 $\frac{13}{4}$, $\frac{23}{2}$ 2 $\frac{23}{7}$, $\frac{34}{14}$ 3 $\frac{12}{8}$, $\frac{22}{16}$

4 $\frac{15}{6}$, $\frac{18}{12}$ 5 $\frac{31}{10}$, $\frac{22}{5}$ 6 $\frac{26}{18}$, $\frac{17}{9}$

7 $\frac{13}{3}$, $\frac{19}{9}$ 8 $\frac{19}{7}$, $\frac{26}{14}$ 9 $\frac{22}{12}$, $\frac{9}{6}$

10 Three children share a bag of cherries. Sam has 10, which is one fifth. Jamal has $\frac{3}{10}$ and Chang has the rest. How many do Jamal and Chang have?

11 Maya's pocket money is £6 per month. She uses $\frac{1}{4}$ of it on bus fares and $\frac{1}{12}$ on sweets. She spends $\frac{2}{6}$ of it on a magazine. How much does she have left?

12 The baker delivers 60 cakes. Class A gets $\frac{3}{10}$, Class B gets $\frac{3}{5}$. How many are left for Class C?

Explore

Which numbers up to 100 can be divided equally into both thirds and fifths? What about halves and sevenths?

Try another pair, for example quarters and sixths.

Bar line charts

How many dogs had:

1. 3 5 dogs

1 3 puppies
2 5 puppies
3 9 puppies?

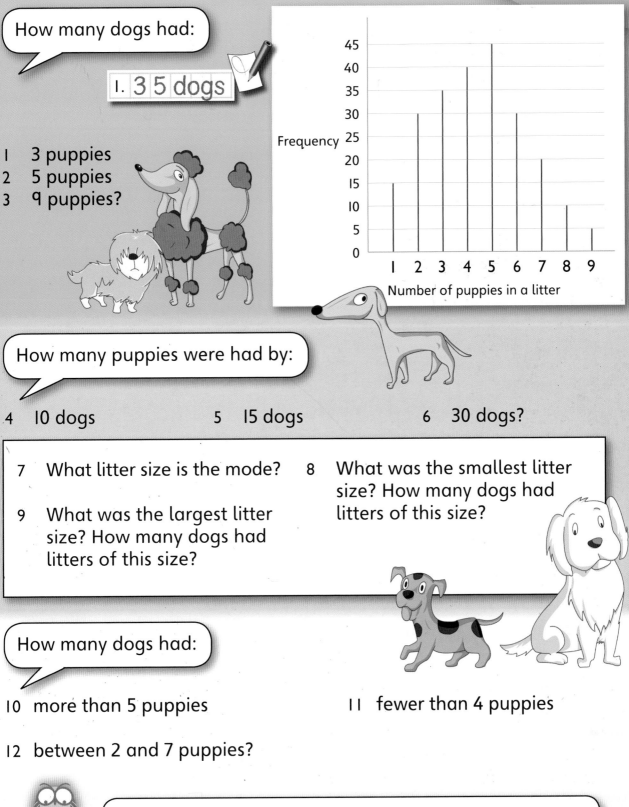

Frequency

Number of puppies in a litter

How many puppies were had by:

4 10 dogs

5 15 dogs

6 30 dogs?

7 What litter size is the mode?

8 What was the smallest litter size? How many dogs had litters of this size?

9 What was the largest litter size? How many dogs had litters of this size?

How many dogs had:

10 more than 5 puppies

11 fewer than 4 puppies

12 between 2 and 7 puppies?

Choose an animal. Sketch a graph to show its litter size.

Bar line charts

Scientists recorded rainy days for I week in March and I week in September, in 100 places. These are their data.

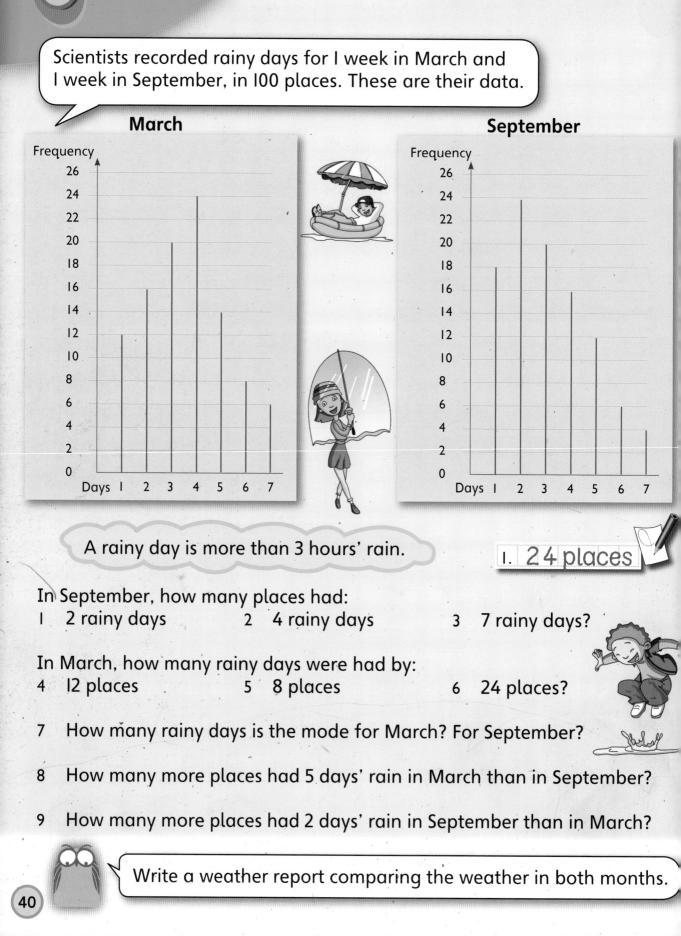

March

September

A rainy day is more than 3 hours' rain.

1. 24 places ✓

In September, how many places had:

1   2 rainy days

2   4 rainy days

3   7 rainy days?

In March, how many rainy days were had by:

4   12 places

5   8 places

6   24 places?

7   How many rainy days is the mode for March? For September?

8   How many more places had 5 days' rain in March than in September?

9   How many more places had 2 days' rain in September than in March?

Write a weather report comparing the weather in both months.

Bar line charts

The calendar shows the temperature recordings for 28 days in October.

Monday	Tuesday	Wednesday	Thursday	Friday	Saturday	Sunday
10°	12°	13°	15°	16°	15°	15°
13°	11°	14°	13°	12°	13°	13°
12°	14°	13°	14°	11°	12°	12°
13°	12°	11°	13°	14°	13°	13°

1 Use the data in the calendar to draw a frequency chart.

Temperature	10°	11°
Frequency	1	

2 Draw a bar line graph to show the data.

Explore

Write six questions about the graph.

Give them to your partner to solve.

You must know the answer!

Horizontal, vertical, parallel and perpendicular

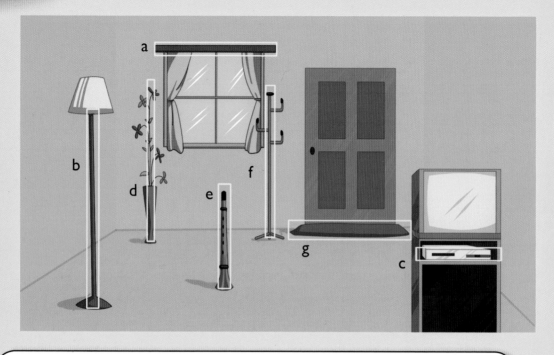

1   For each highlighted object write 'horizontal' or 'vertical'.

1. (a) horizontal

Draw a picture of your own with horizontal and vertical lines. Label them.

2   Copy this pin onto squared paper.

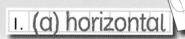

Draw another pin that is:
(a) parallel to it and
(b) perpendicular to it.

3   Repeat for these pins.

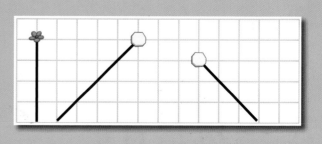

Parallel and perpendicular

Are there parallel lines in these pictures?

I. Yes

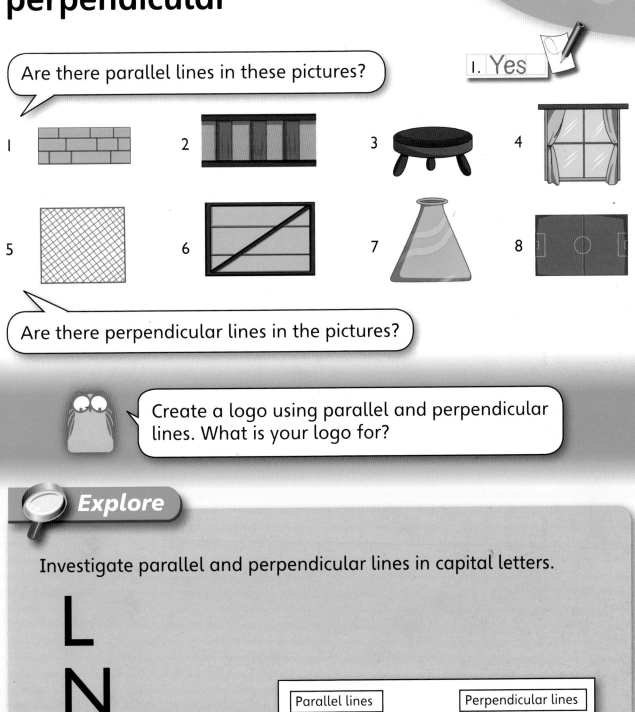

1

2

3

4

5

6

7

8

Are there perpendicular lines in the pictures?

Create a logo using parallel and perpendicular lines. What is your logo for?

Explore

Investigate parallel and perpendicular lines in capital letters.

L
N
H

Draw a Venn diagram to show the results.

Parallel lines   Perpendicular lines

Parallel and perpendicular

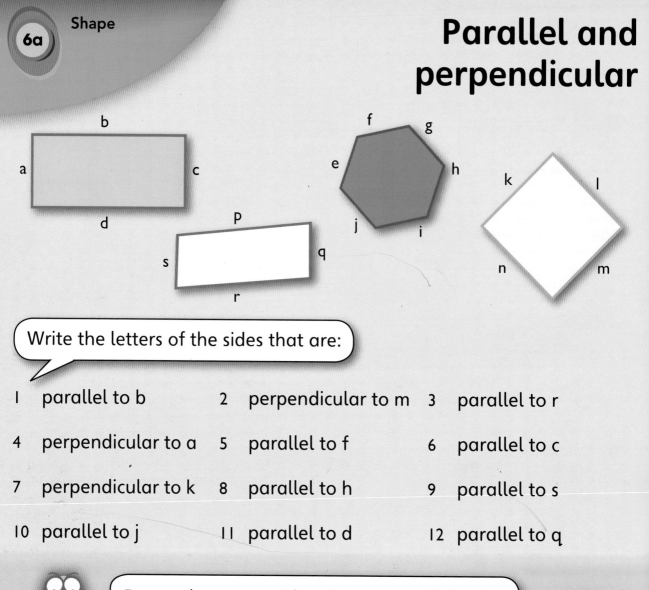

Write the letters of the sides that are:

1 parallel to b

2 perpendicular to m

3 parallel to r

4 perpendicular to a

5 parallel to f

6 parallel to c

7 perpendicular to k

8 parallel to h

9 parallel to s

10 parallel to j

11 parallel to d

12 parallel to q

Draw a hexagon with only two parallel sides.
Try to draw one with three parallel sides

True or false?

13 All rectangles have 2 pairs of parallel sides.

14 If a square has horizontal sides then it also has vertical sides.

15 A regular hexagon has three pairs of parallel sides.

16 The angle between a horizontal line and a vertical line is a right angle.

17 A regular pentagon has perpendicular sides.

18 An equilateral triangle has perpendicular sides.

Parallel and perpendicular

1 Does the shape have parallel sides? If yes, write the number of pairs of parallel sides

1. (a) Yes

2 Does the shape have perpendicular sides?

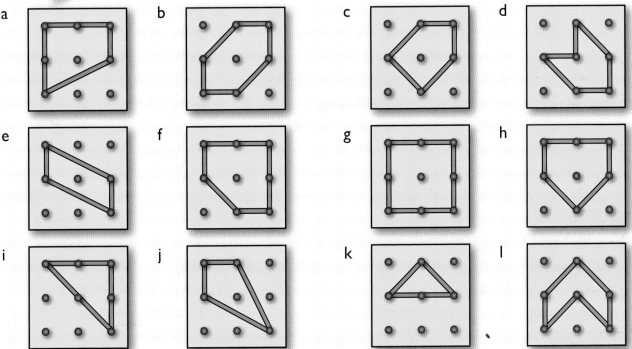

a b c d

e f g h

i j k l

Explore

Draw 4 × 4 squares on squared paper.

Investigate how many different shapes you can draw that have:
- 1 pair of parallel sides
- 2 pairs of parallel sides
- 3 pairs of parallel sides

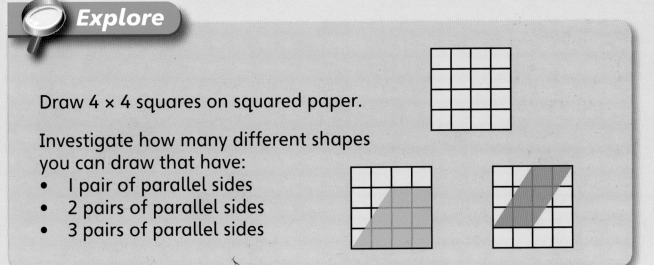

45

Right-angled triangles

1 Copy each triangle and mark its right angle.

1.(a)

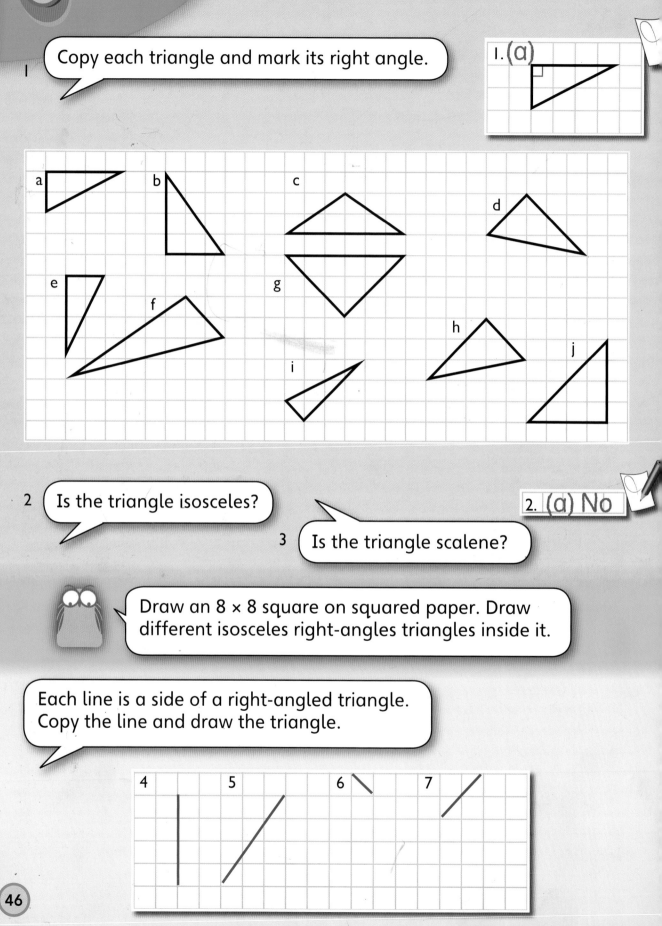

2 Is the triangle isosceles?

2. (a) No

3 Is the triangle scalene?

Draw an 8 × 8 square on squared paper. Draw different isosceles right-angles triangles inside it.

Each line is a side of a right-angled triangle. Copy the line and draw the triangle.

4   5   6   7

Triangles

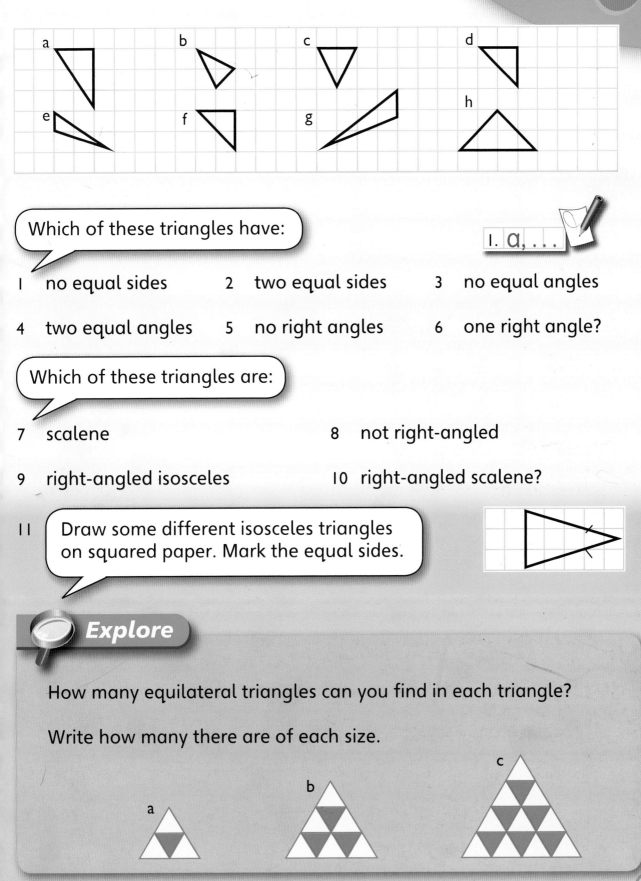

Which of these triangles have:

1. a, . . .

1   no equal sides   2   two equal sides   3   no equal angles

4   two equal angles   5   no right angles   6   one right angle?

Which of these triangles are:

7   scalene   8   not right-angled

9   right-angled isosceles   10   right-angled scalene?

11   Draw some different isosceles triangles on squared paper. Mark the equal sides.

Explore

How many equilateral triangles can you find in each triangle?

Write how many there are of each size.

47

Triangles

1 Write the name of each triangle.

1. (a) right-angled scalene

Choose from:

isosceles   scalene   equilateral

right-angled scalene   right-angled isosceles

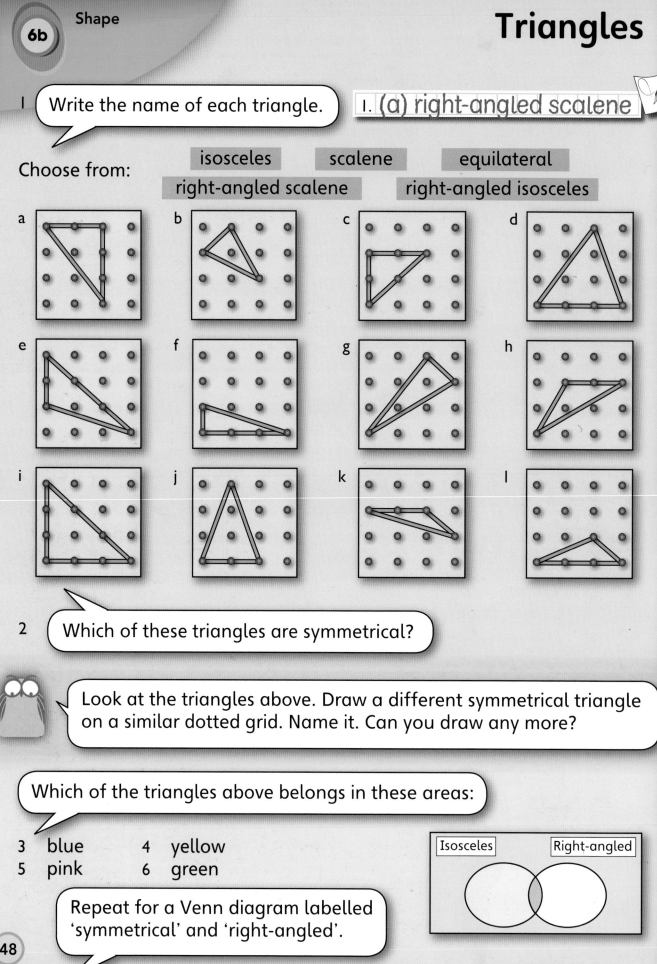

2 Which of these triangles are symmetrical?

Look at the triangles above. Draw a different symmetrical triangle on a similar dotted grid. Name it. Can you draw any more?

Which of the triangles above belongs in these areas:

3 blue   4 yellow
5 pink   6 green

Isosceles		Right-angled

Repeat for a Venn diagram labelled 'symmetrical' and 'right-angled'.

Triangles

True or false?

1 A triangle cannot have more than one right angle.

2 Equilateral triangles have three equal angles.

3 A scalene triangle cannot be right-angled.

4 An isosceles triangle can be split into two equal right-angled triangles.

5 Isosceles triangles are always symmetrical.

6 Right-angled triangles are never symmetrical.

Explore

Draw a large square, then draw its diagonals.

Cut it out, then cut along the diagonals
to make four triangles.

Investigate triangles you can make with:
- two triangles
- three triangles
- four triangles

Name each triangle.

Investigate other shapes you can make.

Name them and draw their lines of symmetry.

Look at each flower and write the number of lines of symmetry.

1. |

1
2
3
4

5
6
7
8

Copy each polygon. Draw any lines of symmetry.

9.

9
10
11

12
13
14

15
16
17

Draw a polygon with no lines of symmetry. Describe it to your partner. Can your partner draw it?

Symmetry

Look at each picture. Which lines are lines of symmetry?

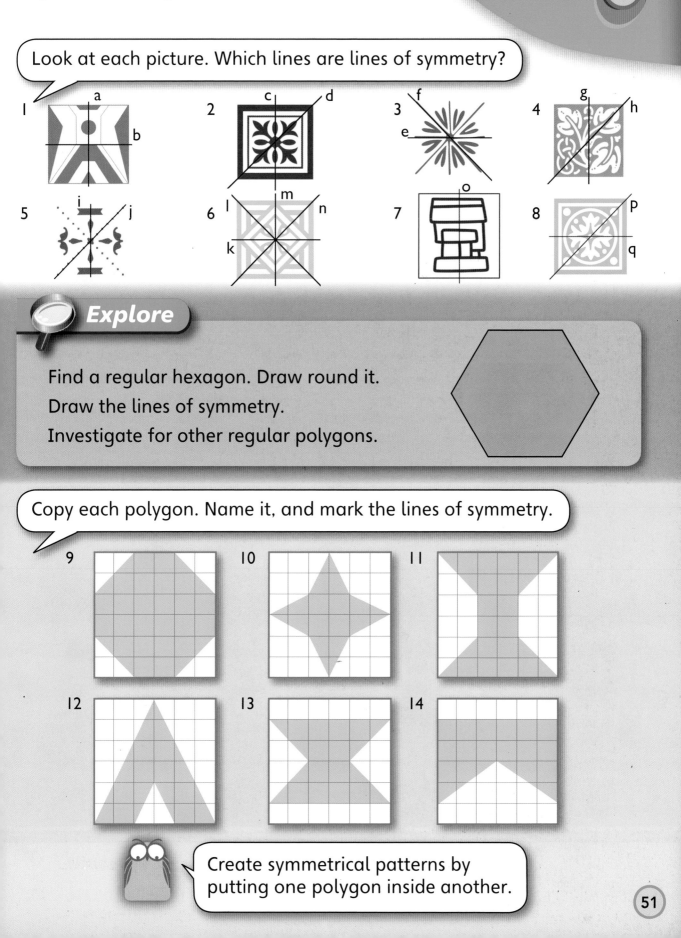

Explore

Find a regular hexagon. Draw round it.

Draw the lines of symmetry.

Investigate for other regular polygons.

Copy each polygon. Name it, and mark the lines of symmetry.

Create symmetrical patterns by putting one polygon inside another.

Symmetry

Copy and complete the pattern each time.
It must be symmetrical in both lines.

1 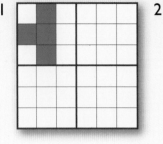   2 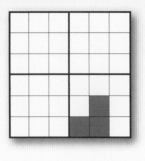   3 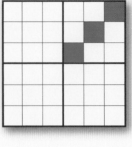   4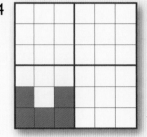

Write how many lines of symmetry on each square.

5   6   7   8

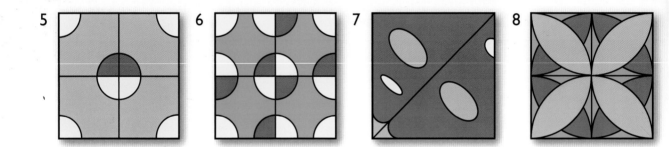

Explore

Draw these two lines on a square.

Rotate or reflect it to create a symmetrical pattern.

Try different patterns.

Predict if they will be symmetrical.

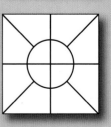

Symmetry

Draw the shape you will see reflected in the mirror line.

1 2 3 4

5 6 7 8

Draw your own pattern to reflect in a mirror line.

Explore

Draw a pair of axes as shown.

Plot three points A, B, C.

Join the points to create a triangle.

Work out where to plot the points on the other side of the axis to create a mirror image

Repeat for a different triangle.

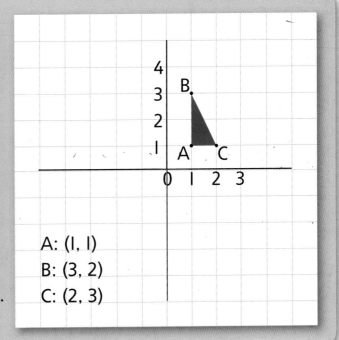

A: (1, 1)
B: (3, 2)
C: (2, 3)

3D shapes

Name each shape. Write the number of faces.

1. cube
   6 faces

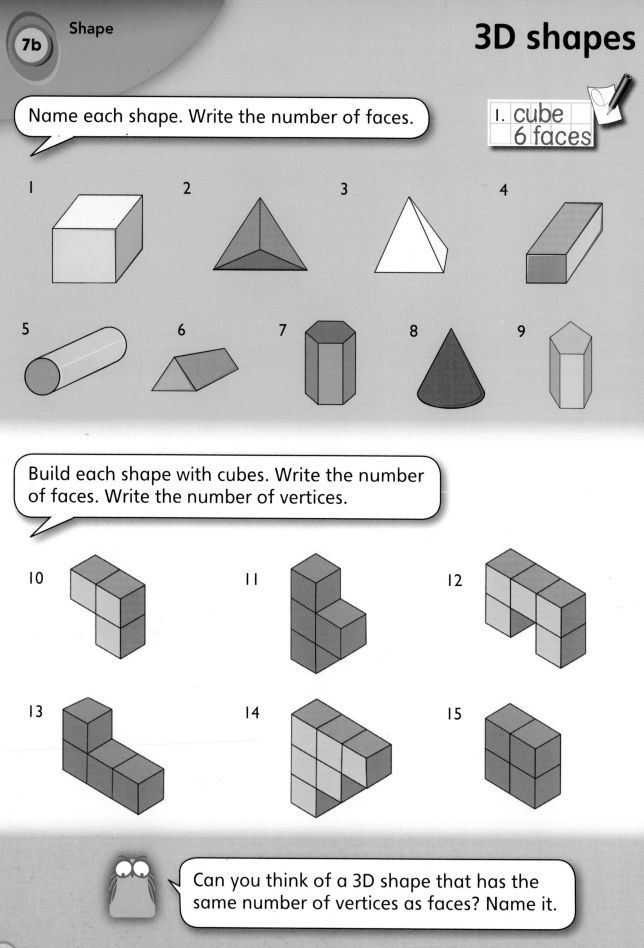

Build each shape with cubes. Write the number of faces. Write the number of vertices.

Can you think of a 3D shape that has the same number of vertices as faces? Name it.

3D shapes

1 Complete the table. Use solid shapes to help you.

Polyhedron	Faces	Vertices	Edges
Tetrahedron	4		
Square-based pyramid			
Cuboid			
Triangular prism			
Hexagonal prism			
Hexagon-based pyramid			

Euler's special number
Add the faces and the vertices. Subtract the edges.

True or false?

2 A cone is not a polyhedron.

3 A triangular prism has more faces than a cube.

4 A cuboid has the same number of edges as a cube.

5 A hexagonal prism has the same number of vertices as a hexagon-based pyramid.

3D shapes

Write the shape each net will make. Choose from the labels.

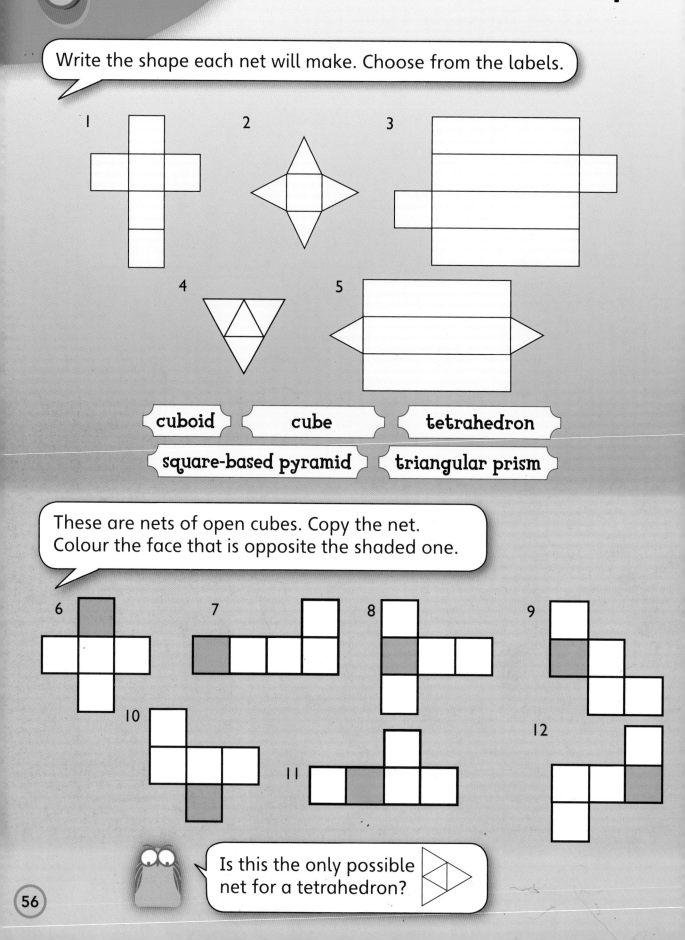

1

2

3

4

5

cuboid   cube   tetrahedron

square-based pyramid   triangular prism

These are nets of open cubes. Copy the net.
Colour the face that is opposite the shaded one.

6

7

8

9

10

11

12

Is this the only possible
net for a tetrahedron?

Metres, centimetres and millimetres

Write each measurement in centimetres.

1. 1·1m = 110cm
   0·9m = 90cm

1 1·1 m 0·9 m

2 1·6 m 1·2 m

3 1·2 m 0·8 m

4 1·3 m 0·7 m

5 1·4 m 0·6 m

6 1·7 m 1·1 m

7 1·4 m 0·9 m

8 1·8 m 1·2 m

Write these in metres.

9 130 cm   10 260 cm   11 80 cm   12 370 cm

Write each door-handle measurement in millimetres.

13 13 cm

14 14 cm

15 12·8 cm

16 13·6 cm

17 12·4 cm

18 8·1 cm

19 14·2 cm

20 15·1 cm

Find some objects in the classroom that can be measured in millimetres. Write their measurements.

Kilometres, metres, centimetres and millimetres

Write each measurement in centimetres.

I. 150 mm = 15 cm
160 mm = 16 cm

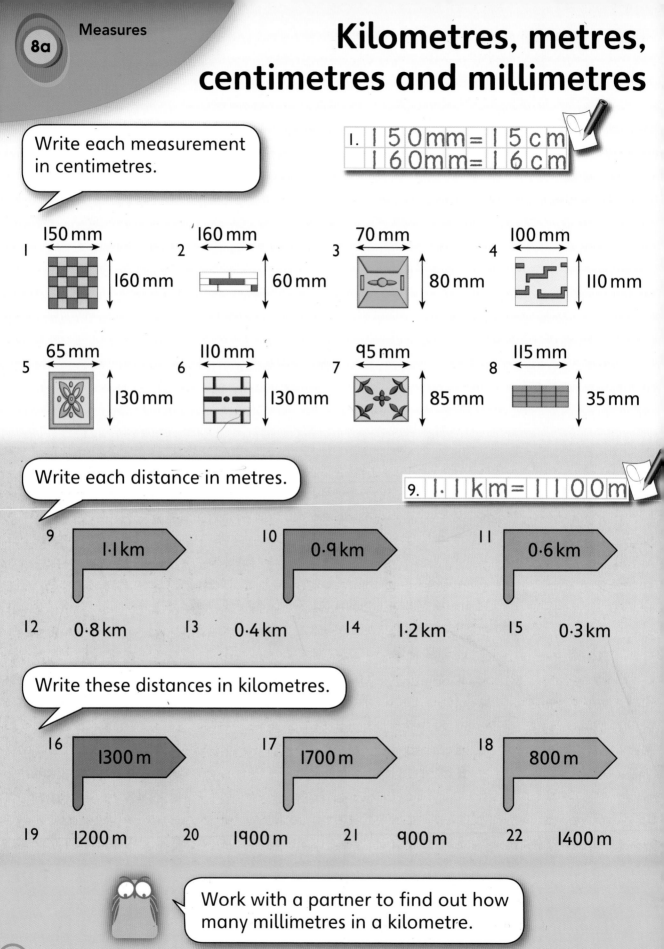

1 150 mm / 160 mm

2 160 mm / 60 mm

3 70 mm / 80 mm

4 100 mm / 110 mm

5 65 mm / 130 mm

6 110 mm / 130 mm

7 95 mm / 85 mm

8 115 mm / 35 mm

Write each distance in metres.

9. 1·1 km = 1100 m

9 1·1 km

10 0·9 km

11 0·6 km

12 0·8 km

13 0·4 km

14 1·2 km

15 0·3 km

Write these distances in kilometres.

16 1300 m

17 1700 m

18 800 m

19 1200 m

20 1900 m

21 900 m

22 1400 m

Work with a partner to find out how many millimetres in a kilometre.

Kilometres and miles

1 Write each distance in miles.

1. (a) 1 6 k m = 1 0 miles

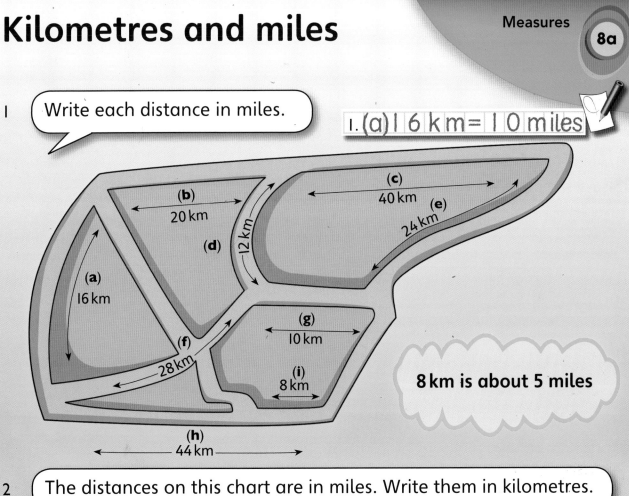

(b) 20 km

(c) 40 km

(e) 24 km

(d) 12 km

(a) 16 km

(g) 10 km

(f) 28 km

(i) 8 km

(h) 44 km

8 km is about 5 miles

2 The distances on this chart are in miles. Write them in kilometres.

Aberdeen

Aberdeen	Aberystwyth	Barnstaple	Birmingham	Brighton	Bristol	Cambridge	Cardiff	Carlisle
500	Aberystwyth							
600	200	Barnstaple						
400	100	200	Birmingham					
600	300	200	200	Brighton				
500	100	100	100	200	Bristol			
500	200	300	100	100	200	Cambridge		
500	100	100	100	200	50	200	Cardiff	
200	200	400	200	400	300	300	300	Carlisle

About how far are you from each of these capital cities: London, Cardiff, Belfast, Edinburgh? Write your answer in miles and in kilometres.

Kilometres

Copy and complete.

1. $5km = 5000\ metres$

1    $5\,km = \boxed{}\ m$

2    $35\,mm = \boxed{}\ cm$

3    $2\cdot6\,m = \boxed{}\ cm$

4    $104\,cm = \boxed{}\ m$

5    $1114\,mm = \boxed{}\ m$

6    $3\,m = \boxed{}\ mm$

7    $2\cdot5\,km = \boxed{}\ m$

8    $70\,mm = \boxed{}\ cm$

9    $230\,cm = \boxed{}\ m$

10   Every day, Jaswinder cycles 10 km to school and 10 km home again. Each week she likes to cycle 100 miles. How many more miles must she cycle?

11   Each time a pencil is sharpened it becomes 4 mm shorter. Alex's pencil is 25 cm. How many times can he sharpen it before it is less than 5 cm long?

12   The rabbit run is 2·5 m long and 1·1 m wide. The rabbit hops round it 10 times. How far does he travel?

🔍 Explore

Work with a partner.

Juan is running the London Marathon, which is 26·2 miles long.

He ran the first 10 km in 45 minutes, and keeps the same speed throughout. How long will he take to complete the race?

Grams and kilograms

Write the appropriate weight.

1. 850g

1 85g 850g 8kg

2 300g 35g 3kg

3 5kg 500g 500kg

4 10g 100g 100kg

5 200g 2kg 20kg

6 5g 500g 5kg

Write the number of grams.

7. 1kg = 1000g

7 1kg	8 $\frac{1}{2}$ kg	9 $\frac{1}{4}$ kg	10 $\frac{1}{10}$ kg
11 1·2kg	12 $\frac{3}{4}$ kg	13 1·9kg	14 $\frac{1}{8}$ kg
15 $\frac{3}{10}$ kg	16 0·7kg	17 $\frac{3}{8}$ kg	18 $\frac{9}{10}$ kg
19 2·3kg	20 0·8kg	21 $\frac{7}{8}$ kg	22 1·4kg

You only have $\frac{1}{4}$, $\frac{1}{2}$, $\frac{3}{4}$, and $\frac{1}{10}$ kg weights. Which weights between 1g and 1kg can you weigh?

Grams and kilograms

Write each weight in kilograms.

1. $650g = 0.65kg$

1

650 g

2

250 g

3

470 g

4

1010 g

5

1250 g

6

870 g

7

1650 g

8

720 g

Write each weight to the nearest $\frac{1}{4}$ kg.

9. $800g = \frac{3}{4}kg$

9

800 g

10

450 g

11

900 g

12

600 g

13

200 g

14

700 g

15

300 g

16

100 g

Find $\frac{1}{8}$ kg in grams. Can you find other fractions of a kilogram, e.g. $\frac{1}{5}$?

Grams and kilograms

Write each weight in grams.

1. 1·2 kg = 1200 g

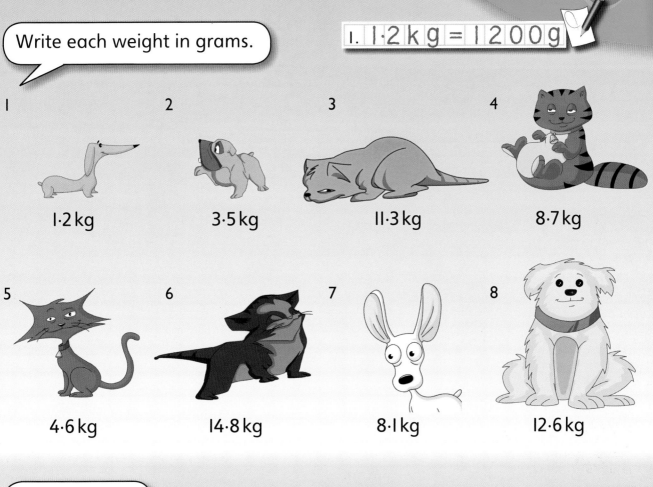

1   1·2 kg

2   3·5 kg

3   11·3 kg

4   8·7 kg

5   4·6 kg

6   14·8 kg

7   8·1 kg

8   12·6 kg

True or false?

9   3 × 350 g is more than 1 kilogram.

10   Each pat of butter is 2 g. There are five lots of 100 pats in 1 kg.

11   5 kilograms is 50 thousand grams.

12   A horse weighs 1001 kg. This is more than one million grams.

13   1 kg of feathers is lighter than 1 kg of coal.

14   1·1 g × 10, multiplied by 100, is more than 1 kg.

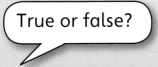 1 tonne = 1000 kg. Work with a partner to find out how many grams there are in a tonne.

Grams and kilograms

The farmer orders twice as much corn as pellets. How much corn does he order?

$1.2 \times 600 = 1200\,g$
$= 1.2\,kg$

1 600 g

2 550 g

3 950 g

4 750 g

5 450 g

6 800 g

7 For dinner, Sam eats 200 g pasta, 100 g mincemeat and 33 g lettuce. About what fractions of a kilogram does he eat in total?

8 The birds on Rashida's bird table eat 300 g seed each day. How many kilograms of seed must she buy each month?

9 Minnie the kitten needs to gain weight. She weighs $\frac{1}{4}$ kg on 1 October and gains 50 g each day. How much does she weigh on 31 October?

Explore

Sunil has six identical-looking weights.

He knows that one weight is lighter than the rest.

He has a balance but no gram or kilogram weights.

What is the fewest number of weighings he must make to find the lighter weight?

Adding

1 **Find pairs of flags that make 100. Write the addition. Do this 10 times.**

1. 50 + 50 = 100

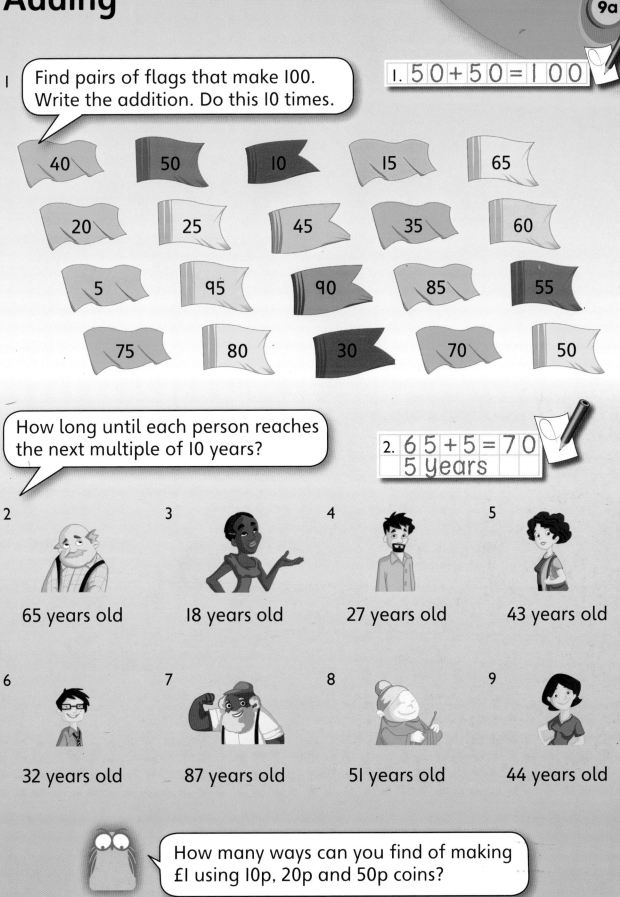

Flags: 40, 50, 10, 15, 65, 20, 25, 45, 35, 60, 5, 95, 90, 85, 55, 75, 80, 30, 70, 50

How long until each person reaches the next multiple of 10 years?

2. 65 + 5 = 70
5 years

2 65 years old

3 18 years old

4 27 years old

5 43 years old

6 32 years old

7 87 years old

8 51 years old

9 44 years old

How many ways can you find of making £1 using 10p, 20p and 50p coins?

Adding

Copy and complete.

1. 42 + 58 = 100

1   42 + ☐ = 100   2   51 + ☐ = 100   3   64 + ☐ = 100

4   58 + ☐ = 100   5   47 + ☐ = 100   6   ☐ + 51 = 100

7   8 + ☐ = 100   8   ☐ + 37 = 100   9   4 + ☐ = 100

10 32 + ☐ = 100   11 ☐ + 28 = 100   12 13 + ☐ = 100

How much change from £1?

13. 65p + 35p = £1
    35p change

13 65p

14 46p

15 54p

16 62p

17 37p

18 28p

19 41p

20 57p

21 73p

22 34p

23 22p

24 77p

How many pairs of numbers that add to 100 contain a 4 digit, e.g. 34 + 66?

Adding

Copy and complete.

1. $5{\cdot}8 + 4{\cdot}2 = 10$

0 1 2 3 4 5 6 7 8 9 10

1 $5{\cdot}8 + \square = 10$

2 $6{\cdot}2 + \square = 10$

3 $4{\cdot}8 + \square = 10$

4 $5{\cdot}3 + \square = 10$

5 $6{\cdot}1 + \square = 10$

6 $\square + 9{\cdot}3 = 10$

7 $\square + 3{\cdot}4 = 10$

8 $\square + 5{\cdot}2 = 10$

9 $2{\cdot}7 + \square = 10$

Each rope was cut from a 10 m roll. How much was left on the roll?

10. $5{\cdot}2$ m

10 4·8 m

11 6·4 m

12 5·7 m

13 4·3 m

14 3·2 m

15 8·1 m

16 2·8 m

17 7·6 m

I have £10 in a bag. There are no notes and no coins less than 50p. There are eight coins in the bag; there are two possible combinations of coins. Find both.

Adding

Each athlete has run part of a 1000 m race. How far left to run?

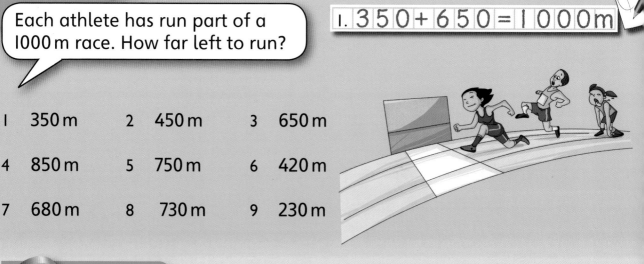

1. $350 + 650 = 1000\,\text{m}$

1	350 m	2	450 m	3	650 m
4	850 m	5	750 m	6	420 m
7	680 m	8	730 m	9	230 m

Explore

Three multiples of 50 total 1000. What could they be?

Can you find all the possibilities?

10 Taife and Joe share 10 kg of dog food. Taife has two dogs so she takes 6.6 kg. How much does Joe have?

11 Ashley squeezes oranges into a litre jug. He uses 10 small oranges to get 780 ml. Roughly how many more oranges will he need to fill the jug?

12 Tanvi has saved £68. How much more must she save to have £100? Her sister has saved £54. How much more does she need?

Work out the number of pounds that must be added to each of these to make £1000: £362, £458, £671, £884. Can you find a quick way of doing this?

Adding

How much to the next hundred?

1. $630 + 70 = 700$

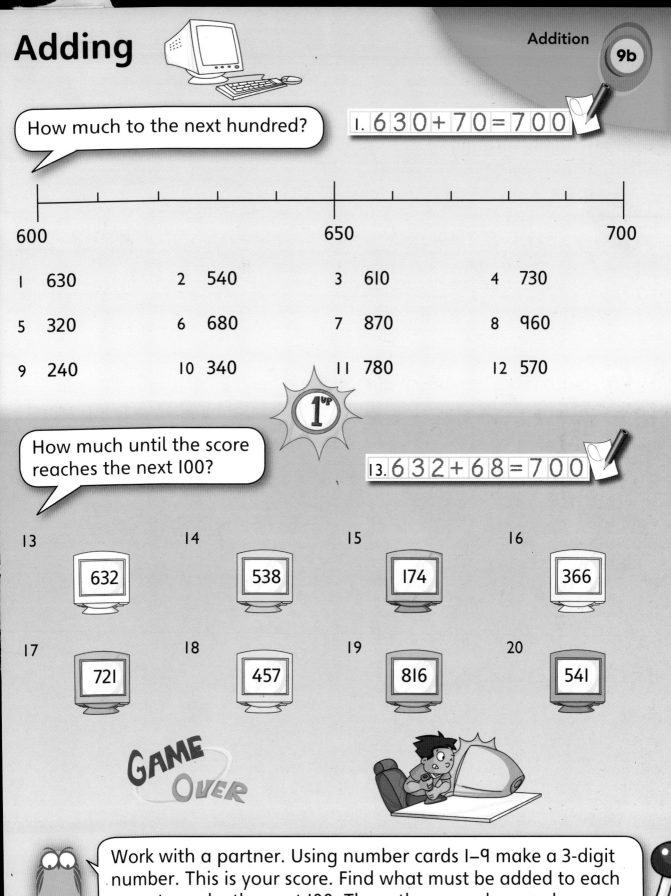

600   650   700

1	630	2	540	3	610	4	730
5	320	6	680	7	870	8	960
9	240	10	340	11	780	12	570

How much until the score reaches the next 100?

13. $632 + 68 = 700$

13	14	15	16
632	538	174	366

17	18	19	20
721	457	816	541

GAME OVER

Work with a partner. Using number cards 1–9 make a 3-digit number. This is your score. Find what must be added to each score to make the next 100. These three numbers make your total score. How can you get the biggest total score?

How far until the mileometer ticks over the next 100?

1. $632 + 68 = 700$

| 1 | 6 | 3 | 2 | | 2 | 7 | 3 | 1 | | 3 | 5 | 4 | 6 | | 4 | 4 | 7 | 8 |

| 5 | 5 | 6 | 5 | | 6 | 4 | 6 | 3 | | 7 | 3 | 8 | 7 | | 8 | 6 | 2 | 8 |

How much more has one child than the other?

9. $£176 + £24 + £4 = £204$
   £28 to save

9 £204 £176

10 £356 £405

11 £482 £508

12 £806 £732

13 £635 £708

14 £243 £304

Take a number with consecutive digits, e.g. 345. How many to the next hundred? Repeat with a new number. What is the pattern?

Adding

Copy and complete.

1. 504 − 488 = 16

1	504 − 488 =	2	606 − 568 =	3	703 − 679 =
4	408 − 379 =	5	507 − 478 =	6	805 − 767 =
7	704 − 667 =	8	603 − 586 =	9	806 − 779 =

10 Work out the cost of the airport tax for each flight.

10. Flight 1: £406 − £368 = £38

Flight	Air fare	Airport tax	Total cost
1	£368		£406
2	£796		£808
3	£466		£507
4	£885		£908
5	£567		£609
6	£676		£709
7	£475		£507
8	£667		£708
9	£588		£609
10	£776		£808

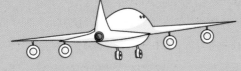

Adding

How many millilitres to the next litre?

1. 638 + 362 = 1000 ml

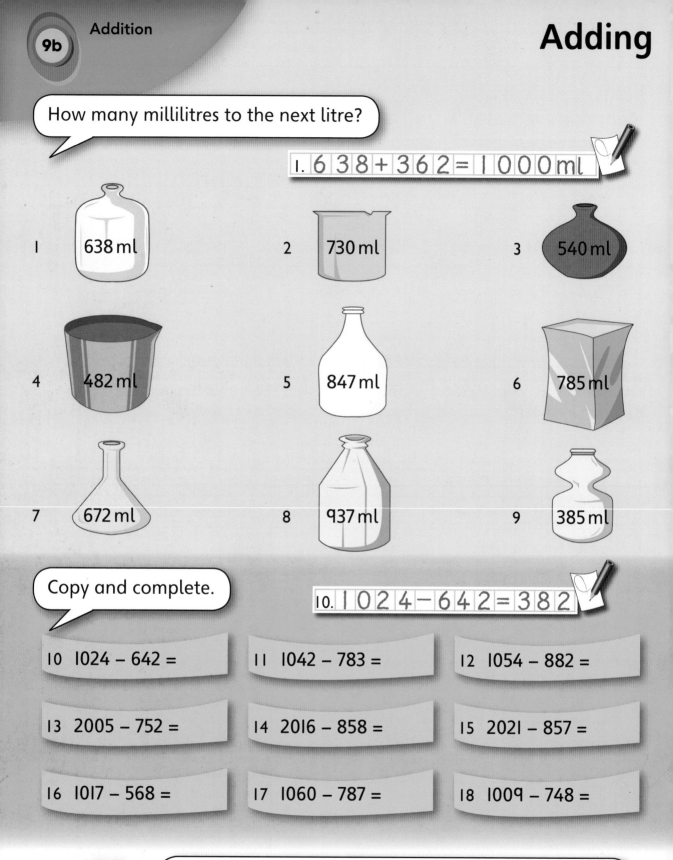

1 638 ml

2 730 ml

3 540 ml

4 482 ml

5 847 ml

6 785 ml

7 672 ml

8 937 ml

9 385 ml

Copy and complete.

10. 1024 − 642 = 382

10 1024 − 642 =

11 1042 − 783 =

12 1054 − 882 =

13 2005 − 752 =

14 2016 − 858 =

15 2021 − 857 =

16 1017 − 568 =

17 1060 − 787 =

18 1009 − 748 =

A 3-digit number with three consecutive digits is subtracted from another 3-digit number, ending in 4. The answer is 226. What could the two numbers be?

Even and odd

Write 'even' or 'odd' for each number.

1. 3 6 3 odd

1	363	2	431	3	669	4	572	5	314
6	863	7	27	8	627	9	3754	10	625
11	6427	12	354	13	32	14	78	15	281

16 Use the card numbers. Write five pairs with an even total. Write five pairs with an odd total.

16. 11 + 29 = 40 even

11

36

24

29

18

47

How many even numbers are there between 1 and 100? Is it the same for even numbers between 101 and 200?

Even and odd

Write a number between 50 and 100 to make each addition work. Write a different number each time.

1. 64 + 22 = even

1 64 + ⭐ = even   2 72 + ⭐ = odd   3 55 + ⭐ = odd

4 48 + ⭐ = even   5 31 + ⭐ = even   6 83 + ⭐ = odd

7 27 + ⭐ = even   8 34 + ⭐ = odd   9 67 + ⭐ = even

Now write the answer to each addition.

Create a new number to match the label by rearranging the digits.

10. 7 4 2 8
    4 8 2 7 odd

10 7428   11 3361   12 494   13 3312

    odd   even   odd   odd

14 9274   15 418   16 5852   17 632

    odd   odd   even   odd

18 183   19 6947   20 2367   21 5437

    even   odd   even   even

How many 2-digit numbers are there between 1 and 100 where both digits are even? Is it the same when the digits are both odd?

Even and odd

1 Use these numbers. Write five pairs of numbers with an even difference. Write five pairs of numbers with an odd difference.

1. $38 - 34 = 4$ even

38

21

34

16

57

45

Write 'odd' or 'even' to complete the statements.

2. even + even + even = even

2 even + even + even = ☐

3 even + odd + odd = ☐

4 odd + odd + odd + odd = ☐

5 even + even – odd = ☐

6 even + even + odd = ☐

7 odd + odd + odd = ☐

8 odd + even – even = ☐

9 even – even – even = ☐

10 even – even – odd = ☐

11 odd + even + odd + even = ☐

12 even + even – even = ☐

13 odd – odd – even = ☐

How many numbers between 200 and 300 have two even digits?

Even and odd

Write each number in figures. Rearrange the digits to create the number closest to the original that matches the label.

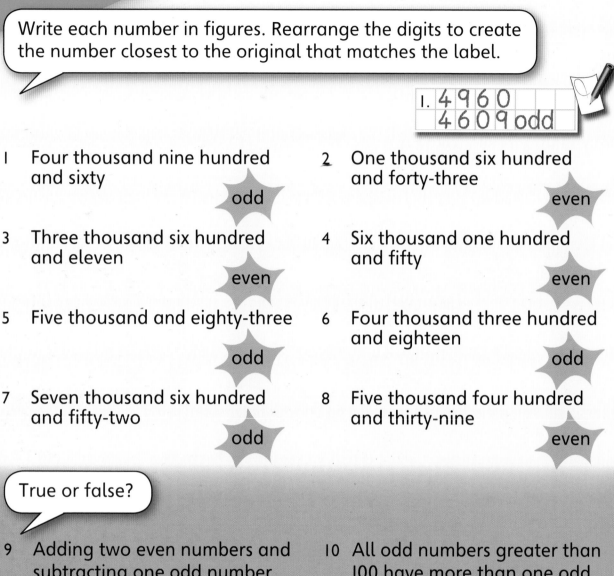

1. 4 9 6 0
   4 6 0 9 odd

1 Four thousand nine hundred and sixty

   odd

2 One thousand six hundred and forty-three

   even

3 Three thousand six hundred and eleven

   even

4 Six thousand one hundred and fifty

   even

5 Five thousand and eighty-three

   odd

6 Four thousand three hundred and eighteen

   odd

7 Seven thousand six hundred and fifty-two

   odd

8 Five thousand four hundred and thirty-nine

   even

True or false?

9 Adding two even numbers and subtracting one odd number always results in an even answer.

10 All odd numbers greater than 100 have more than one odd digit.

11 More months have an even number of days than have an odd number of days.

12 Every even number has at least one even digit.

13 Adding two odd numbers and subtracting an even number always gives an odd number.

14 In the next decade five years will have odd numbers.

How many numbers between 1 and 1000 have an odd digit?

Number sequences

Continue each sequence for four more numbers, counting in 25s.

1. 125, 150, 175, 200

1 0   25   50   75   100

2 900   925   950

3 175   150   125

4 625   650   675

5 13   38   63

6 124   149   174

7 256   231   206

8 27   52   77

Write the difference between pairs of numbers in each sequence. Write the next three numbers.

9. 20 − 16 = 4
   24 − 20 = 4
   36, 40, 44

9 16 20 24 28 32

10 7 10 13 16

11 21 26 31

12 54 60 66

13 22 27 32

14 21 15 9

15 12 9 6

16 10 7 4

Count up in 8s, starting at 0. How many steps does it take to get over 100? How about over 200?

77

Number sequences

Continue each sequence for five more steps.

1. 90, 115, ...

1 | 15 | 40 | 65 | | | | | |

2 | 15 | 30 | 45 | | | | | |

3 | 11 | 22 | 33 | | | | | |

4 | 144 | 132 | 120 | | | | |

5 | 16 | 32 | 48 | | | | | |

6 | 8 | 15 | 22 | | | | | |

7 | 38 | 32 | 26 | | | | | |

8 | 17 | 22 | 27 | | | | | |

Find the smallest positive number that started each sequence.

9.
$$47 - 32 = 15$$
$$32 - 15 = 17$$
$$17 - 15 = 2$$

9   32, 47, 62, 77, ...

10   17, 22, 27, ...

11   22, 28, 34, ...

12   19, 25, 31, ...

13   23, 27, 31, ...

14   38, 43, 48, ...

15   29, 32, 35, ...

16   31, 34, 37, ...

In which of the following sequences does the number 272 occur: counting on in 17s from 0 or in 18s from 0? Write two more sequences starting at 0 that contain the number 272.

Number sequences

Write the first ten steps of each group of three sequences.

1. 0, 3, 6, 9, 12, 15, ...

1   0, 3, 6, 9, ...
    0, 30, 60, 90, ...
    0, 300, 600, 900, ...

2   0, 4, 8, 12, ...
    0, 40, 80, 120, ...
    0, 400, 800, 1200, ...

3   0, 6, 12, 18, ...
    0, 60, 120, 180, ...
    0, 600, 1200, 1800, ...

4   0, 9, 18, 27, ...
    0, 90, 180, 270, ...
    0, 900, 1800, 2700, ...

Continue each sequence for five more steps.

5. 7·2, 7·1, ...

5   7·6, 7·5, 7·4, 7·3, ...

6   3·5, 3·6, 3·7, ...

7   $2, 2\frac{1}{2}, 3, 3\frac{1}{2}, ...$

8   $4\frac{3}{4}, 5\frac{1}{4}, 5\frac{3}{4}, 6\frac{1}{4}, ...$

9   1·71, 1·81, 1·91, ...

10   $5, 4\frac{3}{4}, 4\frac{1}{2}, 4\frac{1}{4}, ...$

11   2·3, 3·3, 4·3, ...

12   $4, 5\frac{1}{2}, 7, ...$

13   4·2, 4·4, 4·6, ...

14   $3, 3\frac{1}{4}, 3\frac{1}{2}, ...$

15   23, 27, 31, ...

16   38, 43, 48, ...

17   29, 32, 35, ...

18   31, 34, 37, ...

Write the sixth, seventh and eighth numbers in a sequence. Ask your partner to find the first positive number in the sequence.

Number sequences

Find the difference between the numbers in each sequence. Write the missing numbers, and the next five numbers in each sequence.

1   100, 89, 78, ☐, 56, ...

2   $4\frac{1}{3}$, ☐, $3\frac{2}{3}$, ...

3   $5\frac{1}{2}$, ☐, ☐, ☐, $6\frac{1}{2}$, ☐, 7, ...

4   3·3, ☐, ☐, 3·6, ...

5   $1\frac{3}{4}$, ☐, $3\frac{1}{4}$, ☐, $4\frac{3}{4}$, ...

6   4·2, ☐, ☐, 7·8, ...

7   $4\frac{2}{3}$, ☐, ☐, $5\frac{2}{3}$, ...

8   3·05, ☐, ☐, 3·08, ...

Invent two missing number sequences, one using fractions, the other using decimals.

Explore

(a)   6, 1, 6, 1, ...

(b)   3, 7, 1, 5, 9, 3, 7, 1, ...

(c)   8, 8, 8, 8, ...

(d)   9, 5, 1, 7, 3, 9, 5, ...

These sequences involve adding 2-digit numbers.

These are the units digits in each sequence.

What could the step size be? For example, the answer to (a) could be adding 25. What else could it be?

Create a sequence like this of your own. Ask your friend to tell you the step size.